SKY MONK

R.R. SHARATH SINGH

Disclaimer

Foreword

Writing *Sky Monk* has been an incredible journey, one that would not have been possible without the unwavering support and love of many remarkable individuals.

To Jane Catherine, my wife, your belief in me and constant encouragement has been the foundation of this endeavor. Thank you for absolutely everything.

To my amazing team, your dedication and hard work during my absence have been inspiring. You have delighted our customers and upheld our values with grace and excellence.

To my family and clients, your love and support mean more to me than words can express. You have been my pillar of strength throughout this journey.

A special thanks to Aakash, the publishing manager at Notion Press, and Unnati Aggrwal, my editor, for your invaluable contributions and guidance.

Finally, to every single person who has embarked on their self-development journey with me, attended a workshop, picked up this book, or shared their experiences within this amazing community—thank you. Your stories and growth inspire me every day.

With gratitude,

R.R. Sharath Singh

Contents

1

Why This Book?

The theme of the book, summarized in one sentence, is to guide individuals to become better human beings. The Bhagavad Gita, Bible, and Quran are religious texts representing different traditions (Hinduism, Christianity, and Islam, respectively). They all share common themes and teachings that promote love, respect, and compassion while guiding individuals to become better human beings.

When Mark Zuckerberg asked Steve Jobs what he should do to become successful, he was stunned by the answer. Steve Jobs told him to go to an ashram in India! What does an ashram provide that a business school doesn't?

Steve Jobs did recommend Mark Zuckerberg visit an ashram in India, specifically the Kainchi Dham Ashram in Nainital, which Jobs had visited in the 1970s. Ashrams offer a spiritual retreat, focusing on self-discovery, inner peace, and personal growth. They provide a disciplined lifestyle away from external distractions, allowing for deep reflection and meditation. In contrast, business schools focus on academic and professional skills, often neglecting the inner peace and mental clarity crucial for genuine success.

Every species on this planet wishes to grow and evolve. Human beings are no different, and the very fact that you're holding this book shows your desire to grow in life. Every human is inspired by people around them and wishes to grow in their career for economic benefits, material benefits, and spiritual benefits.

Everyone aspires to grow but often lacks a clear path or roadmap; hence, they turn to self-help books. These books often end up sitting on the shelf, becoming "shelf-help" books. Why? Because the motivating factor behind growth fades away, and you realize how tough your condition is and how you don't even have time to read the book, despite buying them with good intentions.

If you step into any bookstore, you'll find shelves packed with glossy books promising to make you rich, slim, eloquent, graceful, serene, productive, and stress-free. Essentially, they claim to cover everything under the Sun. And you know what? They're not entirely off the mark. Sure, they might hype things up a bit, but buried within their pages are genuine nuggets of truth.

But here's the kicker: despite these books flying off the shelves and people devouring them, why aren't our lives changing as dramatically as promised? American social physiologist Johnathan Haidt tackled this question beautifully. He likened our bodies and minds to an elephant and its rider, often called the mahout (the person who guides the elephant).

The mahout knows where he wants to go and tries to steer the elephant in that direction— "Go left here, go right there." However, if the elephant isn't trained or simply doesn't want to follow the plan—maybe it wants to snatch some bananas instead—then the mahout can't do much. The elephant is stronger-willed than the mahout; it'll do what it wants.

So, how do you make sure the elephant—your body and mind—cooperate with your plans? Well, it's not by bombarding it with more books, talks, or videos. Instead, it responds to systematic, well-thought-out training and repetition. You have to train both the body and the mind. Others have done it, and so can you, but it takes time, effort, and consistent work. It's not glamorous; it's hard work. And the results? They're nothing short of miraculous.

But here's the thing: we often expect instant results, like wanting the transformative impact of a TED Talk in 20 minutes flat. That's just not realistic. It might take months, even years. You need to give it time and keep at it with unwavering effort. That's the secret sauce to meaningful change.

* * *

Our brain has the amazing ability to change and adapt throughout our lives. This process is called *neuroplasticity*. It means that the brain can reorganize itself by forming new connections between brain cells (neurons). This happens in response to learning, experience, and even injury.

For example, when you learn a new skill, like playing a musical instrument or speaking a new language, your brain creates new pathways to help you master that skill. Similarly, if part of the brain is damaged, other parts can sometimes take over the functions of the damaged area.

Neuroplasticity shows that our brains are not fixed but are constantly developing. This ability to change helps us adapt to new situations, recover from setbacks, and continue growing throughout our lives.

Understanding neuroplasticity can be empowering, as it highlights our potential for continuous learning and personal development. The mind prefers what it knows and is comfortable with. It feels safe with familiar things. On the other hand, it doesn't like things that are new or unknown because they can feel scary or uncertain.

This explains why we often stick to routines and habits, even if they aren't always the best for us. Understanding this can help us nuzzle ourselves to try new things and grow.

Small daily, seemingly insignificant improvements when done consistently over time lead to stunning results. What you do every day brings exceptional results: those tiny triumphs, those micro wins, minor acts of improvement.

A little stretching exercise when you don't feel like doing it, pushing away junk food and eating something healthy, turning off the digital device and picking up the book, getting up a little earlier than later, small little, tiny things when done consistently every single day will bring world-class results and a world-class day.

Be a master of building great days. Great days will lead you to great weeks, great weeks will lead you to great months, great months will lead you to great quarters, and great quarters will lead you to an exceptional year, says one of my favorite authors, Robin Sharma.

If you consistently do harder and harder things, cognitively, emotionally, physically, and spiritually, you keep ongoing to higher and higher levels. I have grown the most during the difficult times. Keep breaking your heart over and over until it opens.

"If there was only joy in the world, we would not learn patience and strength," Robin Sharma.

I want to emphasize the teachings of Jesus Christ, as recorded in the Bible, emphasizing the commandment to love the Lord our God with all our heart, mind, and soul, and to love our neighbors as ourselves. Jesus proclaimed these two commandments as the greatest and most essential for living a life of faith and righteousness.

Loving the Lord our God with all our being means acknowledging and honoring God as the ultimate source of love, truth, and guidance in our lives. It involves developing a deep personal relationship with God and surrendering our hearts and minds to His will. This love for God should permeate every aspect of our lives and be reflected in our thoughts, actions, and choices.

Furthermore, Jesus teaches us to love our neighbors as ourselves. This encompasses loving and treating others with the same care, respect, and compassion that we desire for ourselves. Jesus emphasized the importance of extending love and forgiveness even to our enemies or those who may differ from us. We should extend this love, not only to our families, friends, or those within our immediate communities, but to all of humanity.

By following these commandments, Jesus invites us to transform our lives and the world around us. Loving God allows us to find peace, purpose, and fulfillment while loving our neighbors fosters unity, harmony, and an environment of empathy and understanding. Through these teachings, Jesus reminds us of our interconnectedness and the importance of cultivating love as the driving force in all aspects of our existence.

These texts often emphasize the importance of treating others with kindness, practicing forgiveness, expressing empathy, and leading a moral and virtuous life. They encourage believers to cultivate inner virtues and adopt values, such as selflessness, humility, and generosity.

While the specific narratives and cultural contexts of these texts might differ, the core teachings ultimately converge on the common goal of fostering positive human qualities and encouraging individuals to live in harmony with one another. These texts aim to guide individuals toward spiritual growth and personal transformation, emphasizing the importance of love and compassion as fundamental values for a fulfilling and meaningful life. I thought I should share the knowledge with peace seekers and high achievers in simple language;

My favorite language is Sanskrit, often referred to as "devabhasha" or the language of the gods, and holds a revered status in Indian culture and spirituality. It is esteemed as a divine language, believed to possess inherent power and purity. The letters of the Sanskrit alphabet are known as "Akshara," signifying their imperishable nature. They are considered neither created nor destroyed, existing eternally.

In Sanskrit philosophy, the act of pronouncing Sanskrit words is not seen as a creation, but as a manifestation. When spoken, Sanskrit words do not come into being; rather, they become perceptible or apparent. This viewpoint underscores the idea that Sanskrit is not merely a means of communication, but a medium through which cosmic principles are expressed and manifested.

According to Hindu mythology, the origins of the Sanskrit alphabet are attributed to Brahma, the creator deity. In the Bhagavata Purana, it is narrated that Brahma uttered the Sanskrit letters, which emerged from his mouth. These letters are said to have distinct divisions, such as "svaras" (vowels) and "vyanjanas" (consonants), determined by their pronunciation. This mythological account highlights the divine nature of Sanskrit and its association with creation and cosmic order.

The manifestation of Sanskrit letters from Brahma's mouth symbolizes the divine source of language and knowledge in Hindu cosmology. It suggests that Sanskrit is not a human invention but a divine revelation, reflecting the eternal principles underlying the universe. This belief underscores the profound spiritual significance attributed to Sanskrit and its role in facilitating communication with the divine.

I have used Sanskrit words and phrases in a few places. If I don't use Sanskrit, people will think this guy is making up everything. If I use too much Sanskrit, it just goes above the head and becomes a tough read; hence, I had to strike a fine balance. As per the Bhagavad Gita, he who takes everything from nature and gives nothing back to nature is considered a thief; likewise, he who takes all the knowledge and gives nothing back is also not less than a thief.

Writing this book, giving public speeches, and teaching Gita in my own way have given me knowledge, peace, and bliss. In the Gita, we encounter a pragmatic guidebook offering instructions on how to reshape our thoughts, emotions, and behaviors in our daily lives. By following its teachings, we can tap into a greater reservoir of productivity, enhancing not only our external environment but also enriching our inner subjective experience.

The Gita presents a path of living that fosters social productivity and personal equilibrium, allowing us to navigate life with inner peace. Without this internal harmony and willingness to engage effectively with the external world, individuals may struggle to address their own life challenges successfully.

I would like to thank you for trusting me and having faith in me by buying this book. I am indebted to you. I hope I have done justice and given my best shot. If there are shortcomings, I stand humbly with folded hands and assure you that I will work harder and bring out the best in my next book.

This book is dedicated to the great masters like Swami Vivekananda, Swami Mukundananda, Swami Sarvapriyananda, and all other gurus who are working tirelessly and selflessly for the betterment of society (Loka Kalyana).

The above monks have indeed changed my life, and if you look at it through my lens, it will change your life for good as well. I also call it the mental switch. The switch means a series of activities, acquired knowledge, and discipline practiced every day for high performance and a blissful life. The moment I spoke about the title, all my near ones wanted to know if I had access to that one secret teaching, and life took off.

I am tired of telling everyone; that it's not one teaching or one switch, it's a series of activities, a series of switches turned on and off day in and day out. Let me give you an example. If you have been to the cockpit of an aircraft, you see many switches. It's not like one switch and the aircraft takes off; the pilot will conduct many checks and a series of activities before taking to the sky. And there is an autopilot mode where it's all automated, and the aircraft cruises by itself. Likewise, a series of activities practiced every day consistently is called consistent systematic effort, so that it becomes effortless and the autopilot of your life.

LIFT YOUR HAND UP

The simple act of lifting your hand is incredibly complex. It involves hormones, cells, nerves, and electrochemical signals. Blood flow and oxygenation. Tendons and ligaments, muscles, and bones. And it's almost entirely subconscious. Yet, you can do it with ease.

If someone asks you how it's done, you say it's automated. I have shared a lot of techniques in the book. Immediately after sharing the technique, I throw the question back at you, asking if it is difficult. Yes or No? If you ask me, I will say, Yes and No. Yes, you just put chocolate in your mouth effortlessly. It dissolves in your mouth and gets digested. Let's look at the digestive mechanism of eating chocolate or any other food.

We consume food, which is broken down into small pieces by our teeth and is added primary digestive enzymes from the saliva in our mouth. It then passes into our stomach, where it is churned and more gastric juices are added to it to induce the breakdown of the food consumed. This mixture then passes through our intestines, whose walls absorb the nutrients from the food and deposit them into the bloodstream to be taken all around the body. The blood, when passing through the lungs, also absorbs oxygen that we have inhaled.

So, the blood carries the nutrients and the oxygen essential for the cells in our body to break down the nutrients into packets of energy. Thus, the cells of our body get nutrients and oxygen from the blood, break down the nutrients into energy, and Life is Sustained!!! But like any other mechanism in this universe, every step produces a byproduct in the form of waste.

The food, post-digestion, is excreted from the intestines as stool. We separate impurities in our blood and our kidneys and excrete them as urine. Our skin puts the liquid toxins out as sweat. (Our skin is the largest excretory organ in our body). Sorry for giving you a lengthy explanation. Anything and everything is difficult only if you think it's difficult; otherwise, chocolate just melts in your mouth effortlessly.

When I was young, I used to love sweets and chocolates, especially. When I asked my parents for a chocolate, they used to give me a task: *Go Fill Water*. I needed to work hard for a small piece of chocolate. When I finally had it, it wasn't as satisfying because of the size. It was painful because I had the fear of losing it. I had to share it with my siblings, which was painful, and then I wanted more and more of it, which was also painful.

After I ate the chocolate, it went away forever, even that is very painful. When the chocolate touches the tongue,

I get a flash of pleasure; it's momentary. Neither when the chocolate is in your hand do you feel pleasure, nor when it reaches your stomach do you feel pleasure. The only time you feel the flash of pleasure is when the chocolate is in your mouth; *it's momentary.*

* * *

The Buddhist perspective often emphasizes the notion: "*anityam, anityam* sarvam, *anityam, kshanikam, kshanikam* sarvam, *kshanikam,* shunyam, shunyam, sarvam, shunyam, dukham dukham sarvam dukham" Translated, it conveys the idea that everything is temporary, momentary, empty and suffering. I find myself drawn to this philosophy of emptiness and suffering.

In particular, the concept of the momentary resonates with me. Reflecting on moments, such as indulging in chocolate, I realize that, despite the fleeting happiness they bring. The sensation quickly fades. It's a brief experience, akin to a passing breeze.

To question the very essence of existence, to declare everything as transient and illusory, requires profound contemplation. I'm captivated by this philosophical question, which makes me want to delve deeper into the nature of reality and our place within it. While I may not fully relinquish my attachments to the material world, I am inclined to delve deeper into the quest for emptiness, embracing, the wonder of the unknown.

If you're looking for a single switch to create magical changes, this book won't help you. If you read it without implementing its methods, it won't benefit you. You'll just gather information and continue with life as usual.

In each topic, I have highlighted the master I learned from and provided the name of the book, quoting them extensively. If the subject interests you or if you wish to gain more insights, please grab a copy or an ebook. This is for those who are browsing a few pages at the bookstore to see what the author is up to, or if you have downloaded a digital sample copy and are considering purchasing an online version.

I truly believe the methods and teachings in the book will help you transform and make you the best version of yourself. Flip your inner switch from negative to positive.

Change

"I can't," to "I can."

From failure to SUCCESS.

Hold your head high and say,

"This is the updated and the best version of myself."

To upgrade our version, you need to analyze where we are currently placed. I am a big cricket buff and use a cricket team analogy to understand your current level; I ask the team leader before conducting a workshop about where their team is and what they aspire to be in terms of the cricket team.

Many will say we are like the Zimbabwe team and aspire to be like the Indian team. People, if they know cricket, that means they are struggling badly and need to reach the peak at the earliest. You need to understand where you stand and what you aspire to become with a clear road map toward the same.

I must admit almost everything I have written in this book; you would already know. Before I published the manuscript, I shared it with some close friends, who were already familiar with the topics covered. I am sure most people reading this book will nod. Yes, I am aware of most of the things. I respect my audience's intelligence. Now it will boil down to one thing: implementation of what you have learned with utmost sincerity.

"Our minds are like parachutes; they only function when they are open," suggests that an open mind is vital for learning, growth, and understanding. This metaphor highlights the importance of being open-minded and receptive to new ideas, experiences, and perspectives. Let's elaborate on the significance of this quote and its connection to the teachings of the Srimad Bhagavatam:

1. Open Mind and Learning

An open mind is one that is willing to accept new information, ideas, and view points. It acknowledges that there is always something new to learn, and that personal growth and wisdom come from being open to diverse sources of knowledge.

2. Srimad Bhagavatam's Teaching

The Srimad Bhagavatam, an ancient Hindu scripture, emphasizes that wisdom and knowledge can be gained from anyone, regardless of their age, social status, position, or even species. This concept is rooted in the belief that the source of wisdom is universal and not limited by human attributes or societal hierarchies.

3. Learning from Anyone

The teaching from the Srimad Bhagavatam encourages individuals to recognize that learning opportunities exist everywhere and in everyone. It suggests that wisdom can be found in the words and actions of people from all walks of life, even in unexpected places and beings.

4. The Role of Listening

The act of listening is crucial to this concept. Being open-minded involves not just hearing, but actively listening to what others have to say. By actively listening, one can gain valuable insights and perspectives that contribute to personal growth.

5. Encouragement for Personal Growth

The idea that anyone can be a teacher and that we should be receptive to their teachings is an impetus for personal growth. It encourages individuals to pursue knowledge and wisdom consistently through their daily interactions and experiences.

6. Breaking Down Prejudices

This teaching encourages breaking down prejudices and preconceived notions about who can offer valuable insights. It challenges biases that may lead individuals to dismiss teachings or wisdom based on factors such as age, social status, or background.

7. Promoting Humility

Being open-minded also fosters humility. It implies that no one person or group has a monopoly on knowledge, and we can all benefit from the shared wisdom of others. This recognition promotes humility and a willingness to learn from a variety of sources.

In summary, the quote and the teaching from the Srimad Bhagavatam underscore the importance of an open and receptive mind for personal growth and learning. Being open to the teachings of diverse individuals, regardless of their attributes, is a fundamental aspect of wisdom and the pursuit of knowledge. It encourages us to be active listeners and remain receptive to the valuable lessons that can be found in unexpected places and from various sources.

THIS IS A CAUSE VERY DEAR TO MY HEART

The proceeds from this book will support a special cause. We are committed to promoting menstrual hygiene and environmental sustainability. As part of this mission, we are donating sanitary pad vending and incinerator machines to as many residential all-girls government schools as possible. This is an important step in managing menstrual waste in schools.

The sanitary pad vending and incinerator machines will provide a safe and hygienic way to use and dispose of sanitary pads. This reduces environmental impact and ensures a cleaner, healthier school environment. Our donation supports women's health and empowerment with practical, sustainable solutions.

With these machines, the schools can manage menstrual waste better, preventing non-biodegradable waste buildup and reducing health risks for students. This initiative promotes better hygiene practices and encourages open discussions about menstrual health, helping to break the stigma around menstruation.

We believe our contribution shows how organizations can improve the quality of life for young women and create a more inclusive, supportive educational environment. This donation will benefit hundreds of students, giving them the dignity and comfort they deserve during their menstrual cycles.

We are dedicated to creating a sustainable and health-conscious society, prioritizing the needs of women and girls with care and respect. This initiative is a step forward, and we are honored to be part of this positive change. Please support us in this mission and be a part of this noble cause.

* * *

2

Let's Understand Mind

"The mind is its own place and, in itself, can make a heaven of hell or a hell of heaven."

– John Milton

"Mind exists only in the activity. It does not exist in any place. If the activity ceases, there is no such thing as mind."

– Sadguru

What is this mind? It is the subtle machine fitted within us by God. While the body is the eternal machine, the mind is the internal one. Its function is to generate thoughts, and it profusely engages in this activity throughout the waking state. It continues to work even when we dream. Only in deep sleep does the mind rest. During deep sleep, the mind is at rest, and you experience blissful peace. At all other times, it stays active and creates thoughts incessantly, as per one theory, with which I agree.

"According to *Sri Sri Ravi Shankar*, the mind extends throughout every cell of the body and even 2 inches beyond it. This awareness allows you to sense when someone is approaching, even before they touch you."

Mental health challenges often disrupt inner peace and stability. Buddha was a mind specialist. Buddha demonstrated expertise in addressing these issues, evident in the transformation of some of his followers within the Sravaka Sangha.

Consider *Patachara*, once a prosperous man's daughter, who faced a series of tragedies: losing her husband, her children, and witnessing her family's demise. These adversities shattered her mental well-being, leading to aimless wandering. However, upon encountering a sermon by the Tathagata, her life took a profound turn. Accepted into the sangha, she received guidance in dharma, which gradually healed her mental state.

Similarly, *Angulimal*, notorious for his murderous rampage, ultimately found redemption under the Buddha's guidance. His transformation from a ruthless criminal, symbolized by his garland of fingers, to a member of the sangha, showcased the power of the Buddha's teachings.

Contrastingly, Devadutta, the Buddha's cousin, and Prince Ajatashatru remained unhealed, despite being part of the sangha. Their lack of genuine devotion to the dharma stopped them from recovering. The Buddha emphasized not the individual, but their understanding–bodha. His teachings, such as anapanasati, focused on breath awareness, serving as a means to reconnect with the body and calm the restless mind.

According to Buddhism, the root of many mental health problems lies in avidya, ignorance, leading to likes (raga) and dislikes (dwesha). Through practices like samadhi and prajna, one can transcend these afflictions, gaining insight into truth and embarking on the path of liberation.

Mind also means *Antahkarana* in Sanskrit. The direct English translation of Anthakarna means inner instrument. You may ask, what do you mean by inner instrument? Is there an external instrument? Of course, there are external instruments. The sensory system includes the eyes, ears, nose, tongue, and touch. They are called external instruments because they are in contact with the external world. Eyes are in contact with form, ears with sound, nose with smell, tongue with taste, and skin with touch.

Then there are motor organs: hands for working, legs for walking, and speech for talking. They are in contact with the external world, dealing with the external world. In contrast to this, you have an inner instrument that comprises the mind, intellect, memory, and ego. In Sanskrit, it is called *mana*, *buddhi*, *chicha*, and *ahankara*. All are precisely defined. You will be surprised to know that these are defined.

Use the senses to contact the objects without attachment and aversion (Raga and Dwesha in Sanskrit). The automatic conditioning of objects pulling the senses like a magnet should not happen. The person with controlled senses, that person, can mix with the world, interact with the world, and even enjoy the objects of senses with senses in check. Such a person enjoys the joyful serenity of the mind.

I used the words Raga and Dwesha, the Sanskrit words; meaning attachment and aversion.

Raga (राग):

Definition: Raga, in Sanskrit, translates to "attachment,", "desire,", or "attraction." It represents a strong liking or attachment to something or someone. It is a powerful emotion that can lead to craving and desire.

In Yoga and Vedanta: In these philosophical traditions, "raga" is considered one of the primary obstacles to spiritual growth and self-realization. It is seen as a hindrance because attachments and desires can bind individuals to the material world and prevent them from realizing their true nature.

The Nature of Raga: Raga can manifest in various forms, such as attachment to material possessions, attachment to relationships, or attachment to certain outcomes. It often arises from the ego and the sense of "I" and "mine." It is associated with worldly desires and passions.

Overcoming Raga: In yoga and Vedanta, one of the central goals is to overcome raga by cultivating detachment and non-attachment. Practitioners are encouraged to detach from their desires and recognize that true happiness and liberation come from within, not from external sources.

Dvesha (द्वेष):

Definition: Dvesha translates to "aversion", "hatred", or "dislike" in Sanskrit. It represents a strong feeling of repulsion or avoidance toward something or someone. Dvesha is the opposite of raga.

In Yoga and Vedanta, Dvesha is also seen as a hindrance to spiritual growth. It can create mental and emotional turbulence, leading to suffering and an inability to see the true nature of reality.

The Nature of Dvesha: Dvesha can manifest as hatred, anger, fear, or any form of aversion. It often arises from a sense of threat, discomfort, or past negative experiences. Like raga, dvesha is also associated with the ego as it stems from the identification with the "I" and "mine".

Overcoming Dvesha: In a spiritual context, the goal is to overcome dvesha by cultivating equanimity and understanding. Practitioners are encouraged to examine the root causes of their aversions and to work on transforming them into a more neutral or compassionate perspective. This helps in achieving inner peace and clarity.

In summary, '*raga*' and '*dvesha*' are two fundamental aspects of human psychology discussed in Indian philosophy. Raga represents attachment and desire, while dvesha represents aversion and hatred. Both are seen as obstacles to spiritual growth and are to be overcome through practices that lead to greater self-awareness, detachment, and equanimity. By transcending raga and dvesha, individuals can move closer to self-realization and inner peace.

* * *

Let's discuss the mind and its relationship with awareness. Let's consider the mind to be a vast area and the awareness as a bee, using the metaphor of a bee in a vast field and comparing the mind to the bee's choices and actions. Let's elaborate on the analogy step-by-step:

1. The Mind as an Open Vast Field:

The analogy begins by likening the mind to an open, expansive field. This field represents the canvas of one's consciousness where thoughts, emotions, and experiences flow. Just as a field can have diverse areas, the mind contains various thoughts, ideas, and emotions.

2. Awareness as a Bee Seeking Nectar:

In this analogy, awareness is symbolized as a bee. The bee is a metaphor for the conscious mind that navigates the vast field of thoughts and experiences. It moves from one area to another, symbolizing the focus and attention of the individual.

3. The Rose Garden, Sewage, and Filth:

Within the vast field of the mind, two distinct areas are highlighted: the "rose garden" and the "sewage and filth." These represent the contrast between positive and negative thoughts, emotions, and experiences.

Rose Garden: The "rose garden" symbolizes positive, harmonious, and uplifting aspects of one's thoughts and experiences. It's a place of beauty, goodness, and positivity, analogous to seeking happiness and fulfillment in life.

Sewage and Filth: Conversely, the "sewage and filth" represent negative, distressing, and harmful aspects of one's thoughts and experiences. This is akin to dwelling on negativity, resentment, and distress.

4. Choosing the Rose Garden:

The analogy suggests that, like the bee seeking nectar, one's awareness should focus on the "rose garden." It encourages the individual to make the rose garden their permanent base within the mind. This means consistently choosing to focus on positive and uplifting aspects of life despite the challenges and negativity that may exist.

5. Nectar as Positive Contributions to the World:

The bee's collection of nectar from the rose garden represents the positive and constructive actions or contributions one can make to the world. By concentrating on positive thoughts and experiences, individuals can cultivate inner peace, happiness and an ability to make a positive impact on others.

6. Avoiding the "Filth" and Negative Reactions:

The analogy makes a clear distinction between the bee and a fly. The bee seeks nectar and avoids the filth, while the fly is attracted to it. Similarly, the individual's mind should steer clear of negative, harmful, or unproductive thoughts and reactions.

7. The Stink and Intensity of Negativity:

The analogy concludes with a reference to the unpleasantness of negativity. It highlights that negativity, much like the stench of bodily fluids, can be intense and repulsive. However, if one consistently focuses on positive aspects, the impact of negativity is less pronounced.

While on my way to the airport in a taxi, I noticed an unpleasant odor inside the vehicle. Initially, I acknowledged the situation, recognizing that rented cabs can have their pros and cons. I calmly requested the driver to open a window, and the introduction of fresh air and the picturesque countryside scenery had a magical effect, altering the conditions.

However, when we encountered vehicle pollution at a traffic signal, I had to adapt to the circumstances. Had the driver declined my request to open the window, or if the unpleasant odor persisted, making me uncomfortable, I would have opted to avoid the situation by canceling the ride.

In summary, this analogy is a powerful way to convey the importance of directing one's awareness and thoughts toward positivity, even in the face of life's challenges. By choosing the "rose garden" within the mind and making it a permanent base, individuals can cultivate a positive mindset and contribute positively to the world. It emphasizes the idea that our thoughts and focus can shape our experiences and interactions with others.

3

The Misery of Arjun Singh

Bob and Abhimanyu are identical twins with a humble upbringing. It was a normal delivery when Bob was born; however, the parents endured a challenging experience at the hospital during their son Abhimanyu's birth. The mother had to face intense pain, while the baby also encountered difficulties throughout the delivery process.

The birth did not unfold smoothly, posing additional obstacles for everyone involved; hence, his father named him *Abhimanyu*, the fighter. Bob is naturally talented, and Abhimanyu had to really focus and invest his time at home studying books to get a hold of school education, while Bob just passed the exams with good grades effortlessly.

Every night at dinner, Bob and Abhimanyu's father, Arjun, the head of the family, would ask them, "What did you learn today?" Both boys had to share something new they had learned. If they said, "We didn't learn anything," their father would respond, "Come, let's learn something and make the most of today," before sitting down to eat.

This routine turned Abhimanyu into a curious learner, while Bob enjoyed making up stories during dinner. Later in life, Bob secured a job at a software company through campus recruitment. Abhimanyu, however, didn't get selected and decided to take the tougher route. He attended many interviews and, after much effort, finally landed a job at a software company.

Abhimanyu continued gaining knowledge while working in a company, whereas Bob turned toward entertainment after office hours. Abhimanyu slowly moved up the corporate ladder and became the youngest manager in a short time, and everyone lauded him for his effort and performance.

Years passed by, and one day Bob's dad, Arjun, was completely ill and bedridden. He knew it was his final few days. One day, while having dinner, he asked his sons, "What did you learn today?" Arjun would often ask his sons.

One day, he said, "I know my time on this planet is coming to an end. Now you may ask me, what did I learn from this life?"

Arjun was a humble and saintly man, respected by society for his principles. He had quit drinking and smoking at a young age, dedicating his life to helping those in need.

Abhimanyu looked at him and said, "Father, please tell us—what did you learn from this life?"

Arjun smiled and said, "Let me share the biggest lesson I learned, the one that changed my life completely. I wasn't always like this. I used to be angry, arrogant, and full of myself.

"One day, everything changed when I met a saintly person. It was a glorious morning. I was at the airport after meeting a client, sitting in the lounge and drinking beer. That's when I noticed a monk next to me. He radiated peace and bliss." The monk, standing at an impressive 6 feet tall, was well-built and draped in a robe. His appearance reminded me of a Buddha statue.

I was drunk and started making fun of him.

"What's with the costume?" I teased.

"Why don't you have any hair on your head?"

"Do you ever get confused while washing your face—where to stop?"

He remained calm, smiling gently.

"I can manage. Not a problem," he replied.

I offered him a beer.

"No, thank you," he said. "I'm good with water."

I laughed and said, "Eat, drink, and be merry—it's written in the Bible!"

He said, "Eat, drink, and be merry" is a phrase found in the Bible, specifically in the King James Version (KJV) of Ecclesiastes 8:15. Here's the verse:

"Then I commended mirth because a man hath no better thing under the Sun than to eat, and to drink, nd to be merry, for that shall abide with him of his labor the days of his life, which God giveth him under the Sun."

Ecclesiastes stands out as one of the captivating "Wisdom Books" within the Old Testament, cherished for its profound insights into the human condition. Often hailed as containing the poetry of the Hebrew nation, Ecclesiastes delves deep into existential pondering, inviting reflection on life's purpose and the enigmatic mysteries of God.

Western commentators have long debated the essence of Ecclesiastes, grappling with its apparent ambivalence toward life. Does it convey a positive or negative outlook? Interestingly, many find parallels between its reflective tone and the philosophical depth of the Upanishads, making it somewhat relatable for Indian audiences.

At the heart of Ecclesiastes lies a clinical and philosophical examination of existence, delving into the mysteries of God and offering wisdom on how to navigate life's complexities with grace and wisdom.

However, some of its phrases, like "Eat, drink, and be merry," have been misinterpreted and detached from their context to imply a hedonistic pursuit of pleasure. Yet, a closer look reveals a more nuanced message. Ecclesiastes acknowledges the fleeting nature of human existence and encourages embracing the simple joys of everyday life as a source of comfort and meaning.

The famous passage enumerating the various seasons of life serves as a stark reminder of life's cyclical nature. It encapsulates the ebbs and flows of human experiences, urging us to confront both joy and sorrow with resilience and cheerfulness.

In essence, Ecclesiastes offers a profound inspiration: despite life's uncertainties, it advocates for a gratitude-filled approach, recognizing God's hand in every blessing.

It reminds us that amidst life's transience, God remains the only constant, infusing beauty into every moment and imbuing the human heart with a longing for eternity.

Arjun shared his experience with his sons.

"I was shocked when it hit me—it felt like a wake-up call. I quickly settled my bill and checked the flight status. By then, I had sobered up and realized how wrong I was to make fun of the monk. I wanted to apologize, so I started looking for him, but he was nowhere to be found."

"Soon, it was the final boarding call for my flight. Feeling guilty, I had no choice but to board. As I walked to the plane, I kept praying for a chance to see him and say sorry."

"My seat was 7B. When I booked the ticket, I had been drunk and accidentally chosen a middle seat—the one I hated the most. Now, as I approached my seat, the guilt of disrespecting the monk was still weighing on me."

"I glanced toward seat 7A, and to my surprise, the monk was sitting there! His face lit up when he saw me, and he greeted me warmly. I was stunned by his reaction, but also incredibly relieved. Finally, I had the chance to apologize for what I had done."

* * *

4

The Monk Who Changed My Life

Arjun approached the monk and said, "I was looking for you everywhere."

The monk replied, "I was also looking for you."

Surprised, Arjun asked, "For what?"

The monk smiled and said, "I wanted to say goodbye and wish you a wonderful journey."

Arjun's eyes welled up as he said, "You are such a great man, and I hurt you. I am extremely sorry for my actions."

The monk stopped him gently. "Hold on. Sorry for what?"

Arjun confessed, "I purposely made fun of your appearance."

The monk said calmly, "You had your doubts, and I clarified them. What is there to take as offensive?"

Arjun then asked, "Can I call you Master?"

The monk replied warmly, "Yes, you may call me anything you like, dear Arjun."

The Master continued, "One essential aspect of happiness and fulfillment for every individual lies in the realm of human relationships. The quality of our relationships often shapes the joy we derive from life, much like organizing one's home.

"Many of our relationships require nurturing or healing. This could mean apologizing where we've gone wrong or forgiving those who've caused us pain. Lingering resentment and bitterness corrode our thoughts and well-being.

"Reconciling conflicts, making amends, or showing kindness, even to rivals, can bring glorious rewards. While forgiveness can be difficult, it holds the transformative power to mend and restore relationships."

"Forgiveness is the greatest lesson I have learned from Jesus Christ."

Walking in the "newness of life" necessitates a shift in thought patterns. Within each individual resides a realm comprising their thoughts, desires, and aspirations—an internal kingdom where joy or sorrow takes root. As cautioned by biblical wisdom, safeguarding one's heart diligently is paramount, for it determines the course of one's life.

Just as a wheel requires oiling to maintain smooth functioning, so do our friendships demand attention and care. Instances of feeling low or isolated are universal experiences, wherein the longing for love and recognition remains profound. During such moments, nurturing the inner spirit becomes imperative. Those who extend compassion in such times serve as angels. Our thoughts wield immense power—they shape our destiny, influencing whether we rise or fall.

Throughout life, individuals navigate a complex web of relationships that significantly impacts their overall well-being. Negative emotions harbored in one relationship can contaminate attitudes toward others, thereby subtly shaping one's personality. Despite the technological advancements facilitating communication, authentic and meaningful connections are becoming increasingly rare.

Regrettably, interpersonal relationships remain unparalleled in importance for fostering a compassionate community. Individuals focused solely on self-interest, nurtured in competitive environments, must transition toward collective well-being for the betterment of society. Pursuing selfish aims may lead to loneliness and unfulfilment, whereas extending a helping hand to others fosters reciprocal fulfillment. Each person expands or contracts based on their inclination to withdraw into isolation or reach out to the broader world.

Arjun Singh was visibly stressed as he explained his situation. "I'm under a lot of pressure. I need to close a high-profile sale. My wife is pregnant and alone at home. My elderly parents need care. Layoffs are happening in my office, and I'm worried about my job. Meanwhile, my friends are waiting at the airport to take me straight to a party. If I go, my wife will be furious. Seeing your peaceful life makes me want to leave everything behind, become a monk, and meditate in the Himalayas. I've been considering this for a while. Today feels like the right time. Please guide me, master."

Hearing this, the master's expression changed. His face turned red, and his serene smile vanished. I thought to myself, *Even monks can get angry.*

The master's voice was firm as he said, "You just admitted you have a pregnant wife and aging parents who rely on you, yet you want to abandon them? That's cowardice! You think running to the Himalayas will solve your problems? You wouldn't last a day there. The silence will suffocate you, and you'll wish for your so-called 'stressful' life back."

Even as his anger flared, the air hostess arrived with a glass of water he had requested. I braced myself, expecting him to snap at her interruption. Instead, he turned to her with a calm, genuine smile, thanking her politely. Then, just as quickly, he turned back to me, his face once again stern.

"Do you think God will bless you for abandoning your responsibilities?" he continued. "No. God will condemn you for leaving your loved ones in hardship just to chase some selfish idea of peace in the mountains. True peace comes from facing your challenges, not running away from them."

Arjun implored the master to show him kindness and gentleness, explaining that if he were to recount the difficulties of his childhood and the problems he was facing currently, it would evoke sympathy and justify his current actions. The master said everyone experiences significant pain during childhood and adulthood, but we perceive everything as problems and develop a problem phobia. It's a challenge, and you can overcome it.

The Master said, "You've been emotionally hijacked, Arjun. It's time for an emotional detox. In my words, you need to empty your cup, Arjun."

5

What is Worry?

Worry is a mental state characterized by anxiety and unease about potential future events. It often stems from a lack of control or uncertainty about what lies ahead. At its core, worry is the absence of trust. When we worry, we are essentially doubting our ability to handle future challenges or the likelihood that things will turn out well. This doubt creates a cycle of negative thinking that can be hard to break.

Trust, on the other hand, is a profound sense of confidence and assurance. It is the belief that, even though we haven't seen the outcome, we know it will be there. Trust is built on faith and experiences that reinforce our belief in positive outcomes. It allows us to let go of our anxieties and embrace a more peaceful state of mind. Trust is the antidote to worry; it reassures us that, despite uncertainties, things will work out as they should.

* * *

Building Emotional Resilience

1. Emotional Detox:

Definition: Emotional detox refers to the process of cleansing and releasing negative emotions, stress, and mental clutter from your life. It involves recognizing, acknowledging, and letting go of emotional baggage that may be weighing you down.

Elaboration: Emotional detox is essential because it allows you to free yourself from the burdens of past grudges, regrets, and unresolved emotions. By detoxifying your emotions, you create space for more positivity, resilience, and inner peace. This process often involves techniques such as mindfulness, meditation, journaling, and seeking professional help when needed.

2. Forgiveness:

Definition: Forgiveness is the act of letting go of resentment, anger, or the desire for revenge toward someone who has wronged you. It involves pardoning the offender and releasing the emotional attachment to the offense.

Elaboration: Forgiveness is a powerful practice that enhances inner strength by liberating you from the emotional burden of holding onto grudges. It allows you to move forward with a sense of freedom and peace, improving your emotional well-being and resilience. Forgiving others, or even yourself, can lead to better mental and emotional health.

3. Gratitude:

Definition: Gratitude is the practice of recognizing and appreciating the positive aspects of life, no matter how small. It involves acknowledging and being thankful for the people, experiences, and blessings in your life.

Elaboration: Cultivating gratitude strengthens your inner resilience by focusing on the positive aspects of life. Gratitude helps shift your mindset from negativity and complaints to positivity and contentment. It boosts your emotional well-being, reduces stress, and helps you see life's challenges in a more balanced and manageable light.

How These Practices Enhance Inner Strength:

Release of Emotional Baggage: Emotional detox and forgiveness help in releasing the emotional baggage that can weigh you down, freeing up mental and emotional energy.

Resilience: By letting go of negative emotions and adopting a forgiving attitude, you build emotional resilience, allowing you to better cope with life's challenges.

Positive Mindset: Practicing gratitude shifts your perspective toward the positive aspects of life, fostering a more optimistic and hopeful outlook.

Reduced Stress: These practices can lead to reduced stress levels, contributing to better overall mental and emotional health.

Improved Relationships: Forgiveness and gratitude can positively impact your relationships, promoting understanding, compassion, and empathy.

In conclusion, increasing your inner strength through emotional detox, forgiveness, and gratitude is a holistic approach to emotional well-being and resilience. These practices help you let go of negativity, promote positive emotions, and build the inner fortitude needed to navigate life's ups and downs with grace and strength. I call this process "empty the cup".

* * *

Master further elaborates on the concept of the 4 pillars - Accept, Adopt, Alter, and Avoid - provides a practical framework for managing stress and coping with life's various circumstances and situations. Let's elaborate on each of these pillars with detailed explanations and examples.

1. Accept:

Definition: Acceptance involves acknowledging and coming to terms with the fact that there are certain aspects of life and situations that you cannot change or control. It is about letting go of resistance and recognizing that not everything will go as per your liking.

Explanation: Acceptance is the foundation of stress management. It means accepting the reality of a situation without dwelling on how things should have been different. It helps to reduce inner conflict and emotional distress by embracing the idea that not everything is within your control.

Example: Imagine you are stuck in a traffic jam, and you have an important meeting to attend. Accepting the situation means acknowledging that you cannot change the traffic or magically make it disappear. Instead of getting frustrated, you accept that delays happen and focus on finding ways to deal with the situation constructively, like notifying your colleagues about the delay or using the time to catch up on emails.

2. Adopt:

Definition: Adoption involves recognizing situations where you have some control but may need to adapt to the conditions or circumstances. It means making necessary adjustments to align with the reality of the situation.

Explanation: Adoption requires a flexible and pragmatic approach. It means being open to change and being willing to accommodate the situation while maintaining your well-being. It's about finding a way to work with what's available.

Example: If you're traveling and your flight gets delayed, adopting the situation means accepting the delay and making the best of it. You might use the extra time to relax, read, or even get some work done. This adaptability reduces stress and makes the situation more manageable.

3. Alter:

Definition: Alteration involves attempting to make changes in a situation that is causing you stress. It implies taking proactive steps to modify the circumstances or environment to better suit your needs and preferences.

Explanation: Alteration is about problem-solving and making changes to improve the situation. It requires a proactive mindset and an understanding that some circumstances can be influenced and changed through your efforts.

Example: Suppose you're feeling stressed at work due to an overwhelming workload. To alter the situation, you might discuss your workload with your supervisor, delegate tasks, or reorganize your work schedule to manage tasks more efficiently. By taking these steps, you can potentially reduce work-related stress.

4. Avoid:

Definition: Avoidance is the last resort and involves recognizing situations that are causing you significant stress and harm, and choosing to distance yourself from them when possible.

Explanation: Avoidance is a strategic decision to protect your mental and emotional well-being. It acknowledges that some situations are not worth the emotional toll they take and that it's better to remove yourself from them when feasible.

Example: If you are consistently experiencing stress and conflict in a toxic relationship or a negative work environment, avoidance could mean taking the step to remove yourself from that situation. It might involve ending the toxic relationship, seeking a new job, or reducing contact with individuals who are a source of stress in your life. If you are not enjoying the ride, feel free to get off the bus.

In summary, the 4 pillars - Accept, Adopt, Alter, and Avoid - offer a comprehensive approach to managing stress and navigating life's challenges. It emphasizes the importance of recognizing and responding to various situations in the most suitable way, whether that involves accepting the unchangeable, adapting to what can be modified, proactively altering circumstances, or, as a last resort, avoiding situations that are detrimental to your well-being. This approach promotes emotional resilience and effective stress management.

* * *

According to American writer Norman Vincent Peale, lack of self-confidence and deep-rooted feelings of self-doubt and insecurity are serious problems that have negatively impacted our lives today. In all walks of life, we come across people "who are inwardly afraid, who shrink from life, who suffer from a deep sense of inadequacy, who doubt their own powers." Some sinister fear constantly haunted them that some unfortunate occurrence is going to take place.

When unable to cope with adverse situations in life, we often hear people making negative statements like "I am finished," or "Life has become a veritable hell for me." This sort of mindset, where one sees no glimmer of hope, is detrimental not only to one's physical and mental well-being but also to the aspirations of youngsters who want to make it big in life.

If a person has been grappling with a difficult situation for a long period without being able to resolve the issue, it is probably because they have told themselves that finding a solution to the problem is next to impossible and that nothing can be done to remedy the situation. Thus, persistent negative thoughts create a groove in the brain, influencing one's actions and thoughts, often against our wishes.

Prince Arjuna, as depicted in the Bhagavad Gita, embodies the archetype of the confused and distressed youth found universally. Within him, we see reflected the common affliction of the younger generation: a pervasive fear of perceiving situations and events as problems, even when they may not be. This tendency to interpret occurrences as insurmountable obstacles leads to a sense of despair. Indeed, this phenomenon, labeled as "problem phobia," afflicts modern youth worldwide, shaping their outlook and experiences.

Lord Krishna was not spared, and below are the challenges faced by Lord Krishna, yet he always displayed a gentle smile and faced everything he had to face. Here are the challenges faced by Lord Krishna during his childhood:

1. **Threat from his Uncle Kamsa:** Lord Krishna faced the constant threat of his uncle, Kamsa, who was determined to kill him because of a prophecy

that stated Krishna would be the one to bring about his downfall.

2. **Being separated from his biological parents:** Lord Krishna was separated from his biological parents, Devaki and Vasudeva, immediately after his birth. He had to grow up in secrecy, away from their presence.

3. **Living as a cowherd in Gokul:** Lord Krishna was raised in a rural setting in the village of Gokul by Yashoda and Nanda, who were cowherds. Adjusting to a different family and lifestyle would have presented its own challenges.

4. **Battling demons sent by Kamsa:** As a child, Lord Krishna had to confront and defeat various demons sent by his uncle, Kamsa, who wanted to eliminate him. These demons posed physical and spiritual threats.

5. **Balancing his divine nature with his human form:** Lord Krishna, being an incarnation of Lord Vishnu, had to navigate living as a divine being in a human form. Balancing his divine qualities with his earthly experiences would have been a unique challenge.

Despite these challenges, Lord Krishna embraced them with grace and displayed his divine nature through his actions and teachings. His childhood experiences played a significant role in shaping his identity and purpose on Earth. Master said, "I am sure your challenges were bigger than what Lord Krishna faced."

Not only Krishna, but also Lord Jesus faced many hardships. The circumstances of Jesus' birth, from being born in a humble stable amidst the hustle and bustle of a crowded inn to living a life of simplicity and obscurity as the son of a carpenter for 30 years, underscore his deep connection with the human experience. Despite his divine nature, Jesus chose to embrace pain, tragedy, and suffering as integral parts of his mission to heal humanity.

His birth in a lowly stable symbolizes his solidarity with the marginalized and downtrodden. Throughout his life, Jesus showed compassion and empathy toward the suffering and the outcasts of society, demonstrating his understanding of human struggles.

As he approached his inevitable death, Jesus did not shrink from the pain and suffering that awaited him. Instead, he willingly accepted the path of the cross, knowing that it was the fulfillment of his purpose. In his last moments, his humble submission to the will of the Father exemplified his unwavering faith and commitment to his divine mission.

Through his sacrifice on the cross, Jesus paved the way for all humanity to find redemption and salvation.

His death and resurrection symbolize the triumph of love over sin and death, offering hope and eternal life to all who believe in him.

In this light, Christmas takes on a deeper significance. It is not merely a celebration of Jesus' birth, but a reminder of the profound sacrifice he made for the sake of humanity. The humble manager and the rugged cross are intertwined symbols of Jesus' life, ministry, and ultimate victory over death. It is through the lens of the cross that we truly understand the profound meaning of Christmas and the message of hope and redemption that it brings.

* * *

The Master said, "Arjun, you're distracted, anxious, and overwhelmed. It's as if you're trying to escape from yourself. I saw you opening your laptop and pretending to work, then switching to your iPad as if reading, and finally turning to your phone to listen to music."

He continued, "We've lost the ability to simply sit and be present. Blaise Pascal once said, 'All man's miseries derive from not being able to sit quietly in a room alone.' Think about it: when we get in the car, we immediately turn on the radio. At home, the TV goes on the moment we walk in. Even while watching TV, we flip through channels, unable to focus long enough to watch a commercial. Our minds are constantly filled with noise, and we let our attention get pulled in a thousand directions. This habit of constant distraction keeps most people from truly concentrating."

"Stop overwhelming yourself by endlessly switching the channels of your mind. Train yourself to focus on one thing at a time. Exceptional work comes from deep concentration, not scattered effort. When you're fully present, your brainpower and resources will align with your purpose. If you truly focus on what I'm saying, I can guide you toward transformation."

He added, "We lack the wisdom of Krishna or the resilience of Jesus, and that's why so many of us live in distress. Krishna teaches that until we take complete refuge in him with all our hearts, we will remain burdened. Krishna has already declared that he is the soul residing in everyone. By seeking him within ourselves, we can find the peace we're searching for."

The Master smiled and said, "Let me tell you a story. Once upon a time, beyond our ordinary world, there was a mystical white screen. This screen, much like the ones we see in movie theaters, had seen countless stories unfold upon its surface. Comedies, tragedies, action-packed adventures, and thrilling mysteries—all kinds of tales played out on this magical canvas, captivating everyone who watched.

Yet, the screen itself remained calm and still. It didn't laugh at the funny moments, cry during the sad scenes, or get excited during the action. It stayed neutral and open, welcoming every story as if it were just a passing visitor. And when the credits rolled, marking the end of another tale, the screen would return to its pure, blank white—ready for the next masterpiece to begin."

* * *

The Mystical White Screen

Witness to Stories: The screen observes countless stories, representing various experiences and emotions.

Impartial and Serene: It remains unaffected by the events unfolding before it, maintaining its calm and neutrality.

Blank Canvas: After each story ends, it returns to its original state, ready for a new story to begin.

The Soul and Reincarnation

Witness to Lives: The soul experiences multiple lifetimes, each filled with different events, emotions, and lessons.

Impartial Observer: The soul, in its purest form, remains detached from the emotional highs and lows of each life, maintaining its essence.

Cycle of Rebirth: After each life ends, the soul is reborn, starting a new journey with a fresh slate, much like the screen awaiting a new movie.

In essence, the mystical white screen serves as a metaphor for the soul's journey through reincarnation. Just as the screen remains unchanged despite the variety of movies it displays, the soul remains constant and pure, regardless of the different lives it inhabits. Each life, like a movie, is a temporary experience, and once it concludes, the soul is ready for a new beginning, much like the screen turning white again.

But what happens after our lives here on Earth come to an end? It is said that upon death, our souls embark on a journey through the vast unknown. Three paths lie before us, like twists in a grand story arc. The first possibility is that of rebirth, where our souls may inhabit the bodies of humans, animals, or even insects. The second possibility is the cessation of existence - a game over where we only experience one birth and then fade into oblivion.

However, it is the third option that intrigued me the most, for I fervently believe in the concept of reincarnation. Like the ever-turning wheel of life and death, the cycle continues. Souls, like cinephiles, return to the wondrous screen of existence for yet another breathtaking show. This perpetual dance between the realms becomes the ultimate epitome of the soul's evolution and growth.

Imagine, for a moment, the countless movies our souls have acted in. Picture the diversity of characters we have portrayed, the emotions we have experienced, and the lessons we have learned. We have laughed as jesters, fought as warriors, loved as star-crossed lovers, and delved into the darkest depths of the human psyche as villains. We have embarked on quests for knowledge, justice, and redemption, all the while inching closer to enlightenment.

As I reflect upon this grand design, I can't help but appreciate the significance of the white screen that holds our destiny. Much like a movie hall, it is a space where the boundaries of reality blur and the essence of our souls shines through. Each film that graces this screen is an opportunity for growth, understanding, and self-discovery. And just like a captivating story, it leaves an indelible mark upon our souls, shaping us into who we are destined to become.

So, my friend, let us embrace the journey of our souls with open hearts and minds. Let us cherish every moment of this divine movie experience we call life. And when the final curtain falls, know that the screen will once again turn white, offering a clean slate for the next captivating tale to unfold. For, in the end, it is the stories we live and the lessons we learn that truly define the magnificence of our existence.

* * *

I told him, "Please help me master and guide me on the right path toward a serene and spiritual life. Help shape my destiny so that I feel proud of myself on my deathbed." With a serene smile, he answered, "How badly do you need this? Do you have what it takes to find peace and bliss on this planet?"

I will do whatever it takes. Is it at all possible to be amidst life and be absolutely serene and controlled like you? Is it really possible to have a blissful life on this planet? The master said, of course, that is how life is supposed to be; you people have made it what it is. I asked, can you help me? He said, "Certainly; you are very dear to me, Arjun. I will help you."

I said, "I insulted you, but still you say you are dear to me," The master said, "Many people will insult us, but very few will apologize for their actions upon knowing it's inappropriate. Hence, I consider you a very dear one. When we feel suffering, we have the urge to run away from it and fill ourselves up with the junk food, junk entertainment, anything to keep our mind off the pain that is there inside us. It doesn't work. We may succeed in numbing ourselves from it for a little while, but the suffering inside wants our attention, and it will fester and churn away until it gets it."

"We run away from ourselves because we don't want to be with ourselves. Our pain is a kind of energy that is not pleasant. We fear that if we release our diversions and come back to ourselves, the suffering, despair, anger, and loneliness inside will overwhelm us. But if we don't have the time and willingness to take care of ourselves, how can we offer any genuine care to the people we love?"

* * *

In his book *Autobiography of a Yogi*, Paramhansa Yogananda shares the wisdom imparted by his Guru, Swami Sri Yukteswar, who advises, "Forget the past. The vanished lives of all men are dark with many shames. Human conduct is ever unreliable until anchored in the divine. Everything in the future will improve if you are making a spiritual effort now."

These words offer solace and motivation simultaneously. They console us by acknowledging our past mistakes and the inevitability of future errors until we are firmly rooted in the divine. Sri Yukteswar gently reminds us that dwelling in guilt and regret serves no purpose.

Yet, they also encourage us by highlighting our ability to shape our destiny through present spiritual endeavors. This promise finds support in Krishna's counsel in the Bhagavad Gita (2:40), assuring the absence of "unfinished business" and the negation of duality on the path of yoga action.

Often, people perceive destiny as fixed and beyond their influence, using it as an excuse for negligence. However, destiny is a product of our choices, whether made consciously or unconsciously.

But what about the lingering effects of past actions? Can we mitigate their impact? Swami Kriyananda once offered counsel regarding a karmic debt that nearly proved fatal. Following a near-death experience, he advised to focus on strengthening one's magnetism, a protective aura that can lessen the severity of karmic repercussions.

Engaging in spiritual practices enhances our magnetism, shielding us from negativity and altering our destiny's trajectory. By cultivating positive thoughts, exercising strong willpower, and embracing spiritual endeavors, we fortify our magnetism and pave the way for a brighter future. Ultimately, investing in spiritual growth now promises a better tomorrow and stops suffering.

Arjuna's wise decision paved the way to the Bhagavad Gita. When all attempts at negotiation failed and war became inevitable, both the Kauravas and Pandavas sought Krishna's assistance. Duryodhana, representing the Kauravas, arrived first and sat near Krishna's head as he was asleep. Arjuna followed, positioning himself at Krishna's feet. When Krishna woke up, his gaze fell upon Arjuna first.

Duryodhana argued for his right to Krishna's help based on the principle of "first come, first served," given that he arrived before Arjuna. However, Krishna acknowledged both claims. He offered them a choice: one side could have Krishna's formidable army, the Narayani Sena, while the other side could have Krishna himself, unarmed, and not participating in the battle.

Following the ancient code that the youngest should choose first, Krishna offered Arjuna the first choice. Without hesitation, Arjuna chose Krishna. Duryodhana, filled with confidence at securing Krishna's army, underestimated the value of having Krishna himself as an ally.

The story teaches us several important lessons. Firstly, Arjuna's humble gesture of placing himself at Krishna's feet contrasted with Duryodhana's arrogance in positioning himself by Krishna's head.

Secondly, Duryodhana prioritized material victory, while Arjuna chose the path of righteousness and glory. This decision, rooted in values, ultimately led to the Pandavas' success.

Thirdly, Arjuna displayed intelligence by recognizing the importance of strategic thinking and guidance over sheer military power. He understood that Krishna's counsel would be invaluable in defeating the Kauravas.

Lastly, the significance of having a trusted friend and guide like Krishna during times of moral dilemma cannot be overstated. Krishna's guidance to Arjuna on the battlefield took the form of the Bhagavad Gita, enriching humanity with timeless wisdom. All thanks to Arjuna's wise choice.

Regardless of whether one chooses a life of renunciation or remains a householder, the teachings of the Bhagavad Gita offer guidance on leading a balanced life. This entails valuing both spiritual growth and proficiency in worldly matters equally. The Gita frequently emphasizes the analogy of living like a lotus leaf, which remains pure amidst impure surroundings.

In the Gita's opening scenes, Arjuna, a warrior about to engage in battle, experiences inner turmoil upon seeing his loved one's present on the battlefield. This anguish renders him unable to fight despite his warrior status.

Interestingly, although Arjuna is a householder from a warrior caste, he expresses sentiments similar to those of a renunciate, advocating for withdrawal from worldly activities. However, his reluctance to fight stems not from true dispassion, but from confusion and misguided passion.

The Gita explores the debate between action and renunciation, ultimately advocating for righteous action. While renunciation is praised in certain contexts, the Gita emphasizes the necessity of action. It acknowledges that every action has consequences, but suggests that renouncing action entirely is impractical.

Krishna, the teacher in the Gita, advice to lead an active life while remaining anchored in spiritual principles. He emphasizes detachment from selfish desires, rather than a complete cessation of work. Gandhi interpreted this as renouncing the desire for personal gain, which liberates one from the bondage of action. Gandhi frequently expressed his identity as a humble seeker of God.

While deeply inspired by the Bhagavad Gita, he interpreted its teachings differently from the traditional understanding. In the Gita, Lord Krishna urges Arjun to engage in battle, whereas Gandhi advocated for fighting against the British colonial rule through non-violent means, and he succeeded through this means, and he credits Gita for his resilience.

According to the Gita, true detachment involves performing actions with a sense of surrender to the divine, without attachment to outcomes. This attitude renders one unaffected by the consequences of their actions, akin to a lotus leaf untouched by impurities. Thus, the Gita teaches the importance of detachment from desires while actively engaging in one's duties.

In Indian courtrooms, we place our hand on the Gita and take an oath before speaking. If a lesson or two from the

Gita were recited in courtrooms or prisons, I believe it could reduce crime by fifty percent and lead to many cases being withdrawn and settled mutually.

* * *

The master asserts that suffering is an unavoidable part of this world, and anyone claiming to eliminate it entirely is being unrealistic. However, understanding suffering can help reduce its intensity. Let's delve into the three different types of suffering.

1. **Internal suffering with physical and mental illness:** This refers to the pain and distress that individuals experience due to health issues affecting their bodies or minds. Physical illness can include conditions such as chronic pain, diseases, or disabilities, while mental illness may involve disorders like anxiety, depression, or PTSD. Such internal suffering can adversely affect one's overall well-being and quality of life.

2. **External suffering from the neighborhood or world in general:** This type of suffering encompasses various challenges and hardships that individuals face as a result of their surroundings or society. It can include factors such as poverty, violence, discrimination, inequality, or social injustice. These external pressures can significantly

impact individuals and communities, leading to distress, struggle, and a sense of unfairness.

3. **Suffering caused by nature due to bad weather, cyclones, earthquakes, COVID-19, etc.:** This type of suffering refers to the consequences of natural disasters or extreme weather conditions. Examples include the destruction and loss caused by hurricanes, earthquakes, floods, wildfires, or droughts. These events can result in the displacement of people, loss of homes, livelihoods and lives, leading to immense suffering and hardships for individuals and communities affected by them.

It's important to note that these different types of suffering can intertwine and overlap, affecting individuals simultaneously or at different times. Each type of suffering requires attention, support, and empathy to help individuals cope and work toward healing and resilience.

In today's digital age, the pervasive use of electronic devices has led to a significant increase in stress, suffering and anxiety among individuals. Coping with internal suffering, whether it is related to physical or mental illness, can be a deeply personal journey. Here are some general strategies that can help individuals manage and cope with internal suffering:

1. **Seek professional help:** Reach out to healthcare professionals, such as doctors, therapists, or counselors, who specialize in the specific area of suffering you are experiencing. They can provide guidance, support, and appropriate treatment options based on your needs.

2. **Build a support network:** Surround yourself with understanding and empathetic friends, family members, or support groups who can offer emotional support and a listening ear. Sharing your experiences and feelings with trusted individuals can help alleviate the burden of internal suffering.

3. **Take care of your physical health:** Prioritize self-care activities that promote physical well-being, such as maintaining a balanced diet, getting regular exercise, and getting sufficient, restful sleep. Engaging in activities that promote self-care can positively impact mental health and help manage internal suffering.

4. **Practice relaxation techniques:** Explore relaxation techniques such as deep breathing exercises, meditation, mindfulness, or guided imagery. These practices can help manage stress, reduce anxiety and promote emotional well-being.

5. **Engage in activities you enjoy:** Participating in hobbies, creative outlets, or activities that bring joy and fulfillment can provide a sense of purpose and distraction from internal suffering. Engaging in activities you are passionate about can help foster a positive mindset and overall well-being.

Master points out that we're all pushing too hard for attention and success, turning it into a struggle. He suggests that instead of struggling, we should aim for serenity and success. We need to attain success serenely and enjoy the process.

* * *

The concept of struggle and success in life is a profound and universal theme that resonates with people from all walks of life. Let's dive deeper into this idea.

1. Constant Struggles:

Life is often described as a journey filled with challenges and obstacles. From personal issues to societal pressures, we face a multitude of problems on a daily basis. These struggles can range from the mundane, like everyday stressors, to the more significant, such as pursuing one's dreams and ambitions.

2. The Inner Root Cause:

The statement emphasizes that the root cause of most external struggles is internal. It suggests that our attitudes, beliefs, and mindsets often contribute to, or even create, the difficulties we encounter. Our fears, doubts, and limitations can prevent us from effectively addressing and resolving external challenges. This notion highlights the significance of self-awareness and personal growth in managing life's struggles.

3. Identification and Elimination:

To overcome struggles, the first step is to identify their root causes. This involves introspection and self-reflection. It's only when we understand the underlying issues that we can begin to address them effectively. Whether it's breaking free from self-doubt, letting go of harmful habits, or learning to manage stress, recognizing these internal factors is crucial.

4. Time and Energy Drain:

The statement acknowledges that struggles consume our precious time and energy. This is an important insight because it underscores the real cost of unresolved issues in our lives. Struggles can be draining, both physically and emotionally, and they can distract us from our goals, making our lives needlessly difficult.

5. Mental Distress:

Struggles not only impact our time and energy but also affect our mental well-being. When we constantly grapple with problems, it can lead to stress, anxiety, and even depression. This mental distress can further exacerbate the challenges we face, creating a cycle that's difficult to break.

6. The Path to Success:

The statement suggests that to achieve meaningful success in life, one must mitigate these struggles. By addressing the root causes, managing internal conflicts, and finding healthier ways to deal with external challenges, individuals can pave the way for a more fruitful and fulfilling life. Success often becomes more attainable when we free ourselves from self-imposed limitations.

In summary, the struggle and success in life are intricately connected. While struggles are an inherent part of the human experience, they can be mitigated and resolved by understanding their root causes, both external and internal. By doing so, individuals can save time and energy, reduce mental distress and, ultimately, create a path to success that is more in line with their goals and aspirations. Life's journey becomes more manageable and rewarding when we take the time to weed out the inner issues that contribute to our external struggles.

The air hostess tells Arjun that the business class seat he requested while boarding is now ready, and he can move if he wishes. Arjun replies, "I have the privilege of sitting next to the Master. This is the best seat on the plane right now. If I had the chance, I would sit at his feet and listen to his teachings. I am happy with this seat and not interested in the business class seat or any other luxury on offer. Please do not interrupt unless it is absolutely necessary."

6

Master Class

Be blessed to be human, Arjun. I will tell you about the magic of human existence.

As per Vedas, there are 8.4 billion species of life in existence. The species below human beings, such as animals, birds, fishes, insects, and others, do not have evolved intellect as we humans do. Yet they also perform commonplace activities, such as eating, sleeping, defending, and mating. God has endowed human beings with the faculty of knowledge for a higher purpose, so that they elevate themselves, rarely out of his causeless mercy.

God gives upon the soul the human birth. That means we have received a rare blessing which comes in many lifetimes. You are very special. You might be less important at the moment, but nobody can take away the special status.

At the end-of-life journey, either we are burned or buried. Consider you are buried with the tombstone. There will be a birth date and the death date, and one dash to separate the both dates. It will tell the story of how we lived our life, how many lives we touched, what you gave back to the world, society, and nature. Imagine your tombstone with a 'B' for Birth and a 'D' for Death.

In between, you need to add a 'C.' This 'C' stands for the Choices and Changes we make throughout our lives. The universe will present us with opportunities to make better choices and changes. It's up to us to seize these opportunities and make the most of them. The choices we make ultimately define our destiny.

I feel hurt and upset when I see dead bodies taken to the burial ground with people bursting crackers, littering the road with flowers, and causing traffic jams. Can't it be done peacefully? I've donated my body to medical science. If something happens to me, you just need to make one call. My usable body parts will help other patients, and the rest will be donated to medical students. They can even examine my brain and wonder what made me talk so much.

Arjun says, "Master, you will live for over 100 years and share this special knowledge with humanity."

"Yes, I want to have a meaningful dash on my tombstone."

"I want to know about the perfect life you were talking about," asked Arjun

Master said, "First, understand what life is, then you can make it perfect."

A perfect life is a contradiction in terms. Life itself is a state of continuous struggle between ourselves and everything outside. Every moment, we are actually fighting with external nature, and if we are defeated, our lives have to go. It is, for instance, a continuous struggle for food, water, and air. If food, water, or air fail, we die. Life is not a simple and smoothly flowing thing, but it is a compound effect. This complex struggle between something inside and the external world is what we call life. So when this struggle ceases, there will be an end of life. Humanity and divine powers will not let this struggle end, and life will go on.

Arjun says, "This is not helping, master. You mean to say there is no end to struggle and suffering?"

Master said, "Wait, don't draw conclusions just yet. Hear me out completely, then you decide whether this is of help. Understand the secret of life."

Let's get back to your problem and analyze where you stand.

As per Vedas, they have divided the human life cycle into 4 phases, called 4 ashramas, also referred to as 4 pillars of life. The first 25 years of your life are called Brahmacharya, which means celibacy. This is the student phase of life in this ashrama. One is supposed to gain knowledge from his teacher and remain celibate.

The next stage is called Grihastha (25-50 Years). Griha means house. Grihastha means the stage of life when the person is married and has to fulfill all the duties of his wife, children, father, and mother. This is the most important and challenging stage of life. This stage is expected to end at 50. If you notice in Hindu weddings, there are 4 pillars denoting this concept. Under the four-pillar structure, one transforms his life from Bhramcharya to Grihastha.

The third stage is called vanaprastha (50-75 years). Vana means forest. Vanaprastha means going to the forest. This is the stage when the person retires and turns toward the advisory role, gives up all possessions, and enters the forest. A person cannot enter vanaprastha unless and until his sons can earn on their own, and his daughters are married. This ensures that the person completes all his duties toward his family.

Sanyasa is the fourth phase and the last stage of life and may start at 75 years of age. It is to dedicate entirely to spirituality. One has to practice austerities and thus be prepared for salvation. If he follows this stage properly, he will be released from the cycle of birth and death and given space in heavenly abodes. Some people think they can wait until they turn 75 to focus on spirituality, saying, "I'll be spiritual after 75." But it's important to think about God all the time.

After 75, you should fully dedicate your life to spirituality. I conduct seminars for institutions and corporations, Arjun. Many new managers join a company and feel proud and happy when they receive salutes and respect from their subordinates. However, when I interact with them as they retire as MDs and chairmen, they often struggle to transfer their power and retire. They want to hold on to their position and the respect they receive forever.

I have seen this in many family businesses and in politics. Sometimes, the father wants to hold on to power and doesn't hand it over to the son until his death. In other cases, the father wants to hand over the business, but the son is not interested. These conflicts can start and affect the employees and everyone connected with the business.

Let's focus on the challenging part is age 25 to 50 when one has to work and take care of the family. You are a Grihastha. You have completed sanyasatva and moved to Grihastha. Most of the people want to skip this phase and jump to Vanaprashtha, entering the forest, because of challenges they face in life, work stress, family, and other reasons. That's where you stand. I am taking over the advisory role and telling you what one should do.

* * *

"Dharma, Artha, Kama, and Moksha" are 4 fundamental concepts in Hindu philosophy that collectively form the basis of a fulfilling and balanced life. They are often referred to as the "Purusharthas," which means the goals of human life. Here's an explanation of each along with examples:

1. Dharma: Dharma is the moral and ethical duty or righteousness that an individual should follow in their life. It varies from person to person based on their age, caste, gender, and occupation. Dharma guides individuals to act in a just and ethical manner, fulfilling their responsibilities and obligations. For example, a teacher's dharma is to educate their students honestly and diligently, while a doctor's dharma is to provide medical care with compassion and expertise.

2. Artha: Artha represents the pursuit of material wealth, success, and economic prosperity. It encompasses activities aimed at securing one's financial well-being and ensuring the needs and desires of oneself and one's family are met. For instance, a person may work hard in their career to earn a comfortable living, provide for their family, and accumulate wealth for future security. The whole world is running behind Artha and Kama, ignoring Dharma. Lord Krishna says that whenever there's a decline in righteousness (dharma) and an increase in unrighteousness (adharma), He incarnates Himself to restore the balance.

The full verse goes:

"यदा यदा हि धर्मस्य ग्लानिर्भवति भारत। अभ्युत्थानमधर्मस्य तदात्मानं सृजाम्यहम्॥"

It means, "Whenever there is a decline in righteousness and an increase in unrighteousness, O Arjuna, at that time I manifest myself on Earth." It signifies the divine intervention to maintain cosmic order.

3. Kama: Kama is the pursuit of desire, pleasure, and sensual gratification. It includes enjoying the pleasures of life, such as love, art, music, and other sensual experiences. It's about balancing and indulging in worldly pleasures without excessive attachment or obsession. For example, a couple in love may celebrate their relationship by going on a romantic vacation or enjoying a beautiful meal together.

When you single-mindedly chase pleasure, it means you are solely focused on pursuing pleasurable experiences without considering other aspects of life. This can be problematic because pleasure is not a sustainable or reliable source of fulfillment. Over time, constantly seeking pleasure can lead to a decrease in satisfaction as you become desensitized or habituated to pleasurable experiences.

Eventually, you may find that nothing brings you the same level of pleasure as before, and this can lead to disappointment and a sense of emptiness. It is important to seek a balanced and holistic approach to life, considering not just pleasure, but also personal growth, relationships, meaning, and purpose. If you single-mindedly chase pleasure, you will find nothing pleasurable anymore.

Excessive pursuit of pleasure can impact overall life satisfaction in several ways. This needs a bit of explanation, and attention should be paid to the following because the majority of humankind is confused and suffering because of Kama.

Firstly, it can lead to a decrease in the enjoyment derived from pleasurable experiences. When we constantly seek pleasure, we can become desensitized or habituated to it. As a result, the same activities or stimuli that used to bring us joy may no longer elicit the same level of satisfaction or fulfillment.

Secondly, excessive pursuit of pleasure can lead to a neglect of other important aspects of life. When we focus solely on seeking pleasure, we may disregard responsibilities, relationships, personal growth, and other areas that contribute to overall well-being. This imbalance can create a sense of emptiness or dissatisfaction in the long run.

Lastly, the pursuit of pleasure without considering its long-term consequences can lead to negative outcomes such as addiction, financial troubles, or damaged relationships. These negative consequences can further erode overall life satisfaction.

It is important to find a balance between experiencing pleasure and attending to other important aspects of life, such as personal growth, relationships, and meaningful pursuits, in order to maintain a higher level of overall life satisfaction.

4. Moksha: Moksha is the ultimate spiritual goal, representing liberation, self-realization, and freedom from the cycle of birth and death (samsara). It is the pursuit of eternal truth, enlightenment, and oneness with the divine or the universe. Achieving Moksha is considered the highest state of existence, transcending the limitations of the material world. An example of someone on the path to Moksha might be a dedicated yogi who seeks self-realization through meditation and spiritual practices.

These 4 Purusharthas are interconnected, and it is believed that a balanced life involves pursuing them in harmony. By following one's dharma, achieving Artha and

Kama, and ultimately seeking Moksha, an individual can lead a purposeful and spiritually fulfilling life according to Hindu philosophy.

* * *

Arjun says, "Yes, master, this is exactly my problem. I have succumbed to the challenges life has thrown at me. Help me overcome my challenges."

Master said, "Arjun, we must face our fears with courage and not let fear control us. Let me share a story about how I learned this lesson.

When I was new to the monastery, we had aggressive monkeys around. They waited for handouts, and if we didn't give them food, they would chase us. They loved shiny things and often snatched glasses or caps. The only way to get them back was to toss them something else as a trade. One day, I had nothing to give. I was barefoot, the ground was scorching, and as I walked, a large monkey started chasing me. Terrified, I ran.

A senior monk saw what was happening. Instead of running away, he charged toward the monkey. To my amazement, the monkey fled. Later, the monk explained, 'If you keep running, they'll keep chasing. But if you face them with courage, they will back off.' That moment taught me a lifelong lesson: courage can overpower fear.

"Now, Arjun," the Master continued, "I understand your challenges. But for a moment, let's set them aside and reflect on the blessings in your life. Despite the struggles of your childhood, you graduated college with flying colors, secured a job right after, married your college sweetheart, and now you're about to become a father.

"When life feels overwhelming, it's often a wake-up call, reminding you to pause and focus on gratitude. Think about what you have to be thankful for and who deserves your appreciation. Once you start recognizing these blessings, you'll notice how quickly negativity fades. That doesn't mean challenges will vanish, but you'll face them with renewed strength and grace."

The Master paused, then added, "Even Lord Krishna taught us about courage in the face of challenges. Once, Krishna and Balarama were traveling through a dark forest. Back then, there were no shelters for travelers. As night fell, Krishna proposed, 'I'll sleep while you keep watch. When you feel tired, wake me, and I'll take over.'"

Smiling, the Master said, "There is wisdom in this story, but we'll save the rest for another time. For now, focus on your blessings and approach your challenges with courage. You're stronger than you realize."

Krishna went to sleep. Balarama, who kept moving back and forth, encountered a monster in the forest, and the monster screamed at Balarama. Balarama, shaken up by the monster, shrank in size, and the monster became bigger than Balarama. The monster screamed once more, Balarama shrank even further, and the monster became even bigger.

In one last attempt, the monster screamed at Balarama. Unable to withstand the might of the monster, Balarama screamed "Krishna" and fainted. Hearing the call "Krishna," Krishna woke up. Although Balarama had fainted, he mistook Balarama to be sleeping, and Krishna started walking back and forth. The monster, now seeing a new person standing there, screamed at him once more. Instead of being perturbed, Krishna stared at the monster and asked: "What do you want?"

The Courage of Krishna made Krishna expand and the monster shrink. The monster once again screamed at Krishna. Krishna again asked the monster, "What do you want?"

The monster shrank even further, and Krishna expanded even more. In one last attempt, the monster screamed at Krishna, and Krishna again asked the monster, "What do you want?" The monster then shrunk in size.

The epic goes, Krishna takes the monster, ties the knot at the end of his dhoti and places the monster inside. The Sun did rise, and Balarama and Krishna began to walk. And as they were walking, Balarama told Krishna, "You don't know what happened last night. A monster came, and it was threatening us so much."

Krishna gently took the monster out of his dhoti and showed it to Balarama, asking, "Are you talking about this?" Immediately, Balarama says, "But when I saw it, it was so big, but now it has become so small."

The Veda Vyasa, through the voice of Krishna, says that when you avoid what you must face in life, it becomes bigger than you and takes control over you. When you face what you must face, you become bigger than it, and you take control over it.

The monster here is all the challenges we face in life. If you keep avoiding what you must face, these challenges become monstrous and take control over you. Instead, face what you must face, and you become larger than it and gain control over it. Always remember, challenges are there for a purpose, for you to become what you can become. The challenge is to make your dash more meaningful on the tombstone.

Master, this is exactly my problem. I am running away from my challenges. This is helping me in a big way. I feel very happy and painful at the same time. I don't know how to explain. Happy because I can take control of my life.

Painful because my entire life is going to be upside down. I may have to quit a lot of things I love.

The master said, "I understand how you feel. A friend of mine is a goldsmith who does ear piercings. Little girls come to him to get their ears pierced. It's painful, but at the same time, they're excited to try on the beautiful earrings their mothers and older sisters wear. After the piercing, they get to pick out a nice earring. My friend says he often sees the girls smiling and crying at the same time—crying from the pain but smiling with excitement about what's coming. Is it a struggle? Yes, and no. It all depends on how you look at it. Life puts you in situations where there's plenty of hardship. When you feel like giving up, you might wipe away your tears, think about the success ahead, and find the strength to smile."

Arjun said, "Master, you are such a wise soul. Please, tell me the secret to living a happy life. I want to control my anger. I now understand that anger is an enemy of happiness."

The master replied, "Angry young man, let me quote Swami Vivekananda. He said, 'The person who gives in to anger, hatred, or any other strong passion can't accomplish anything. They only harm themselves. It's the calm, forgiving, and balanced mind that gets the most done.'"

SWAMI VIVEKANANDA

Anger Bubble

When I am angry, my whole mind becomes a huge wave of anger. I feel it, see it, handle it, can easily manipulate it, can fight with it; but I shall not succeed perfectly in the fight until I can get down below to its causes. A man says something very harsh to me, and I begin to feel that I am getting heated, and he goes on till I am perfectly angry and forget myself, identifying myself with anger. When he first began to abuse me, I thought, "I am going to be angry." Anger was one thing, and I was another; but when I became angry, I was anger.

These feelings have to be controlled in the germ, the root, in their fine forms, before we even become conscious that they are acting on us. With the vast majority of humankind, the fine states of these passions are not even known—the states in which they emerge from subconsciousness.

When a bubble is rising from the bottom of the lake, we do not see it, nor even when it nearly comes to the surface. It is only when it bursts and makes a ripple that we know it is there. We shall only be successful in grappling with the waves when we can get hold of them in their fine causes, and until you get hold of them and subdue them before they become gross, there is no hope of conquering any passion perfectly. To control our anger, we have to control them at their very roots; then alone shall we be able to burn out their very seeds. Seeds thrown into the ground will never come up, so this anger will never arise.

One moment of anger is enough to ruin your entire life and career. If you visit any jail, you will come across so many people who want to undo that one moment in their life. If you get to talk to people in jail, 90% of them will say, "I did nothing." Because that one moment of anger wave will turn a human into an animal, and in a fraction of a second, you experience the worst situation of your life. When anger pops in, you need to ask, "What is my intention at this moment?" Is it to be angry, sad, mad, or frustrated, or to be calm and able to respond instead of reacting?

Arjun, patience is a virtue, and the golden word is 'wait'. This is not to say that we do not respond. Many times, we have to do something actively to pacify the mind. However, we have to let the head cool down before we come back with a retort. When the head is hot, the tongue works faster than the mind. Once words have left our mouths, they become permanent. We should never make a permanent decision based on temporary emotions.

Arjun said, "Yes, master, I got angry at my wife while boarding the aircraft. I should have spoken to her nicely." Master said, "You became one with anger while scolding your wife. If I had asked you when you were scolding your wife, you would have justified and said you are right and she is wrong. After some time, when the anger fades away, when you are without that anger, you will regret and feel guilty.

If the anger was right, you should never feel guilty about it. You will feel guilty about the negative actions. I should not have spoken so harshly. I should not have yelled at her for caring about me. That anger, which seemed so right and justified at that moment, now does not feel justified at all. It feels wrong. When does it feel right? When you are totally one with it. When does it feel wrong? When it is fading away. The sensitive people will immediately feel guilty after doing something wrong. Those who are not so sensitive they will keep on justifying."

Arjun said, "Master, it always happens to me from morning to night. I keep screaming at people for no reason, speak junk, and regret it immediately."

Master said, "Tell me about your weekly schedule and start on the weekend."

"On weekends, mostly partying, since I work very hard on the weekdays. During weekdays, I go to the office and work very hard."

Master asked, "How do you prepare for the day, which starts the night ahead?"

"At night, I just watch TV. I avoid drinks during weekdays. Before sleeping, I check social media. I like to watch reels; that's the only entertainment I have. In the morning, I wake up, sit, relax for some time with reels and social media, and quickly get ready for the office and leave."

Master said, "It's pretty simple. If you keep consuming digital junk and junk food all day long, the junk will come out of your mouth."

* * *

Life is nothing but days in miniature, suggesting that life can be understood and experienced by observing and reflecting on individual days. It implies that the patterns, experiences, and lessons of a person's life can be found within the smaller units of time, such as the days that make up a lifetime.

This perspective highlights the significance of each day and the choices we make within them. It suggests that by being mindful and intentional in how we live each day, we can gain a deeper understanding of, and make the most of, our lives.

In this context, it becomes important to approach each day with mindfulness, recognizing that even the seemingly ordinary or mundane moments hold value and potential for growth. It reminds us to be present, to appreciate the present moment, and to take responsibility for how we act and make the most of each day.

By reflecting on and learning from our daily experiences, we can gain insights and wisdom that contribute to our overall journey of self-discovery and personal development. It encourages us to recognize that life is made up of a series of interconnected moments and that we have the power to shape our lives and make each day meaningful. Have your dinner as early as possible and do not touch the mobile phone just before going to bed and upon waking up in the morning. I will list out the advantages of having an early dinner and keeping your digital devices away.

There are several potential benefits associated with having an early dinner:

1. **Better digestion**: Eating earlier allows your body more time to digest the food before you go to bed. This can help prevent indigestion, acid reflux, and other digestive issues that can occur when lying down with a full stomach.

2. **Improved sleep:** Having an early dinner gives your body enough time to metabolize the food before bedtime, which can promote better sleep quality. Going to bed on a lighter stomach can also reduce the chances of discomfort or disrupted sleep due to digestion.

3. **Weight management:** Eating earlier in the evening can support weight management goals. Research suggests that eating late at night may lead to weight gain or difficulty in maintaining a healthy weight. An early dinner allows your body to burn off calories from the meal more efficiently throughout the evening.

4. **Increased energy levels:** Having an earlier dinner gives your body more time to process and absorb the nutrients from your meal. This can lead to increased energy levels in the evening and even the next day.

5. **Enhanced metabolism:** When you eat earlier in the evening, it aligns with your body's natural circadian rhythm. This alignment can optimize your metabolism and the way your body processes and stores nutrients.

6. **Improved appetite control:** Eating an early dinner can help regulate your appetite and prevent overeating later in the evening. Research suggests that late-night eating can be associated with higher calorie intake and potentially contribute to weight gain over time.

7. **Better meal planning and portion control:** Having an early dinner can provide an opportunity for mindful meal planning and portion control.

When you eat earlier, you may be more conscious of your food choices and make healthier decisions regarding what and how much you eat.

Ultimately, the benefits of having an early dinner can vary from person to person, depending on individual preferences and lifestyles. It's important to listen to your body and find a mealtime routine that works best for you.

Yes, it is widely recognized that exposure to blue light emitted by digital devices, such as smartphones, tablets, and computers, can disrupt sleep patterns. Blue light has a short wavelength and high energy, which affects the release of melatonin, a hormone that regulates sleep-wake cycles.

Master said, "Arjun, before take-off, the cabin crew made an announcement about keeping the mobile phone switched off or in-flight mode." She said it will interfere with the aircraft system; I know little about it. If you don't keep the digital devices away, it will certainly impact your sleep cycle.

When we use electronic devices, especially in the evening or before bed, the exposure to blue light can suppress the production of melatonin, making it more difficult for us to fall asleep and achieve a restful sleep. This can lead to difficulties in falling asleep, shorter sleep duration, and disrupted sleep quality.

To mitigate the impact of blue light on sleep, there are a few steps you can take:

1. **Limit device usage before bed:** Try to avoid using electronic devices, especially in the hour or 2 leading up to bedtime, to allow your body to increase melatonin production.

2. **Use blue light filters:** Many devices now have built-in settings or applications that reduce the amount of blue light emitted. These filters can help minimize the sleep-disrupting effects of blue light.

3. **Wear blue light-blocking glasses:** These glasses are designed to filter out blue light and can be worn while using digital devices in the evening. They can help reduce the negative impact on sleep quality.

Sleep is the medicine and the energy generator of the body. Actually, when you sleep, the cleansing process takes place in your body. Getting enough quality sleep is essential for overall health and well-being.

Here are a few ways in which sleep can benefit your mind and body:

1. **Improved cognitive function**: Adequate sleep allows your brain to consolidate and organize

information, which can enhance memory, attention, and overall cognitive function. It can also improve problem-solving skills and creativity.

2. **Enhanced mood and emotional well-being:** Lack of sleep can negatively affect your mood, leading to irritability, mood swings, and increased stress levels. Sufficient sleep helps regulate emotions and promotes a more positive outlook.

3. **Strengthened immune system:** Sleep is crucial for a healthy immune system. During sleep, your body produces and releases cytokines, which are proteins that assist in fighting inflammation, infection, and illness. A lack of sleep can weaken your immune system and make you more susceptible to infections.

4. **Restored energy and physical performance:** During sleep, your body repairs and regenerates tissues, including those in muscles, organs, and cells. This helps restore energy levels, improves physical performance, and facilitates muscle recovery after exercise.

5. **Weight management:** Sufficient sleep plays a role in maintaining a healthy weight. Sleep deprivation can disrupt hormone regulation, particularly those involved in appetite control.

It can lead to increased hunger, cravings for unhealthy foods, and a higher risk of obesity.

6. **Improved cardiovascular health:** Chronic sleep deprivation has been linked to an increased risk of developing heart disease, high blood pressure, and other cardiovascular conditions. Quality sleep allows your heart and blood vessels to rest and recover, maintaining a healthy cardiovascular system.

7. **Reduced stress and anxiety:** Sleep deficiency can contribute to higher stress levels and increased anxiety. Quality sleep provides time for relaxation and helps regulate stress hormones, resulting in improved mental and emotional well-being.

To maximize the benefits of sleep, it's important to prioritize sleep hygiene and establish a regular sleep schedule. This includes maintaining a consistent bedtime routine, creating a comfortable sleep environment, managing stress, and avoiding stimulants like caffeine or electronics before bedtime.

* * *

Arjun said, "Master, I have difficulty sleeping. Can you please share some techniques?"

The master answered, "There are many techniques, but the one below works for me. Most days, I work tirelessly hard. By the time the head hits the pillow, sleep blossoms. On a particularly difficult day, I use these techniques."

Counting backward is a common technique used to help calm the mind and induce sleep. Here's a step-by-step guide to how to do it:

1. **Find a comfortable position:** Lie down in your preferred sleep position, ensuring that you are relaxed and ready for sleep.

2. **Take a few deep breaths:** inhale slowly through your nose, hold it for a few seconds, and then exhale through your mouth. Repeat this a few times to help relax your body and mind.

3. **Start the countdown:** Begin counting backward from a high number, such as 100, or 200, in a slow and steady rhythm. Keep your focus on the numbers as you let go of any distracting thoughts.

4. **Visualize each number:** As you count each number, try to visualize the digits in your mind. Picture them clearly, either written out or floating in space. This visualization can help keep your mind centered and prevent it from wandering.

5. **Maintain a relaxed state:** Keep counting backward, allowing each number to lull your mind into a deeper state of relaxation. If you make a mistake or lose track, simply start over from the previous number you remember.

6. **Gradually slow down:** As you continue counting, gradually slow down the pace of your counting. Let each number linger in your mind for a little longer, allowing your body and mind to become progressively more relaxed.

7. **Drift off to sleep:** Eventually, you may find that you naturally drift off to sleep during the countdown. If this happens, allow yourself to embrace sleep and let go of the counting. If you reach the end of your countdown without falling asleep, try repeating the process or explore other relaxation techniques to help you further unwind.

"Remember, counting backward is just one method among many that can aid in falling asleep. Experiment with different techniques and find what works best for you. It's also important to establish a consistent sleep routine and create a sleep-friendly environment to improve the quality and duration of your sleep. Once your mind gets used to counting backward, you need to try a harder step: mix other languages along with English while counting back."

Arjun says, "Understood, master," counting the numbers backward using different languages so that the mind does not get habituated.

Master said, "Arjun, the neurotransmitters like melatonin and serotonin, hormones, enzymes, and other molecules, play crucial roles in the functioning of our body. They are involved in numerous physiological processes, including digestion, metabolism, immune responses, and the regulation of various bodily functions."

* * *

Melatonin and serotonin are both important neurotransmitters that play vital roles in regulating sleep and mood. When you sleep, you need melatonin. When you wake up, serotonin is at your service; melo becomes sero in my language.

1. Melatonin: Melatonin is a hormone that is produced by the pineal gland in the brain. It is primarily responsible for regulating our sleep-wake cycle, also known as the circadian rhythm. Melatonin levels naturally rise in the evening as darkness sets in, signaling to our body that it is time to sleep. Conversely, exposure to light, especially blue light from electronic devices, can suppress melatonin production and make it more difficult to fall asleep.

Melatonin supplements are available over the counter and can be helpful for individuals who struggle with sleep disorders, jet lag, or irregular sleep patterns. However, it's important to use melatonin supplements under the guidance of a healthcare professional, as dosage and timing can vary depending on individual circumstances.

2. Serotonin: Serotonin is a neurotransmitter that regulates mood, emotions, and sleep. It helps to regulate various physiological functions, such as appetite, digestion, and social behavior. Adequate serotonin levels are important for maintaining a stable mood and promoting feelings of well-being, while low serotonin levels have been associated with conditions like depression and anxiety.

Several methods can naturally elevate serotonin levels, including regular exercise, exposure to sunlight, a balanced diet with tryptophan-rich foods (like turkey, bananas, and nuts), and stress management techniques like mindfulness and relaxation exercises.

It's important to note that while melatonin and serotonin are related to sleep and mood, their levels and interactions in the body are complex. If you have concerns about your sleep or mood, it's best to consult with a healthcare professional for a comprehensive evaluation and appropriate guidance.

Master says, "Each of us is uniquely gifted with a different type of intelligence. No one is given merely one form of intelligence. Though there could be one primary or dominant intelligence, all of us are bestowed with multiple intelligences."

I am someone who is an early riser.

* * *

1. **Wake up early:** Set your alarm for an early time that allows you to have a relaxed and unhurried start to your day. Wake up at 4.30 am during bhrama muhurat. Sorry, you asked me to be considerate. You can wake up at 5 am. As soon as you wake up, please do not look at the mobile phone, no WhatsApp, no email, no social media.

2. **Hydrate:** Start your day by drinking a glass of water to rehydrate your body after a night of sleep. You can also have a cup of warm water with lemon for added health benefits.

3. **Exercise:** Engage in some form of exercise to wake up your body and get your blood flowing. This can be a jog, a workout at home or the gym, or even some stretching, yoga, or a sport. I would advise a brisk walk. When you see the Sun God, bow down; he will bless you. If you wish to play a sport, you are free to do so.

4. **Personal care:** Take care of your personal hygiene, including brushing your teeth, showering, and getting dressed for the day. This will help you feel fresh and ready to take on the day.

5. **Mindfulness or meditation:** Spend a few minutes practicing mindfulness or meditation to center yourself and set a positive mindset for the day ahead. This can help reduce stress and improve focus. No news channel.

6. **Plan your day:** Take a few minutes to plan out your day. Review your to-do list, prioritize tasks, and mentally prepare for any important meetings or deadlines. You can check the WhatsApp and email for important work-related information now, but no social media yet.

7. **Pranayama (Prana is life, and ayama means extension)**

Prana is the name of energy that is in the universe. Whatever you see in the universe, whatever moves or works, or has life, is a manifestation of this Prana. The sum total of the energy displayed in the universe is called Prana.

Breathing is such a simple act, but it's a complex world. The inhale and exhale process is life and death. This act is untrained and underrated. There are different types of breathing for different circumstances. Lord Krishna talks highly about Pranayama for mind and stress control. He is so very right. Recently, science and research have confirmed the advantages of doing Pranayama for self-healing and longevity.

The three sorts of motion of Pranayama are one by which we draw the breath in, another by which we throw it out, and the third action is when the breath is held in the lungs, or stopped from entering the lungs. These, again, are varied by place and time. By place is meant that the Prana is held to some particular part of the body. By time is meant how long the Prana should be confined to a certain place, and so we are told how many seconds to keep it there. The result of this Pranayama is Udghata, the awakening of Kundali.

8. **Healthy breakfast**: Make sure to have a nutritious breakfast that provides you with sustained energy throughout the morning. Include foods like whole grains, fruits, protein, and healthy fats.

9. **Daily reading or learning:** Spend some time reading a book, listening to a podcast, or engaging in any activity that promotes continuous learning and personal development.

10. **Review goals:** Take a moment to review your short-term and long-term goals. This will help you stay aligned with your objectives and motivate you to work toward them.

11. **Leave early for work:** Finally, leave your home with ample time to commute to work, allowing for unexpected delays and avoiding the stress of rushing. Strictly, no shouting and screaming from the car at the fellow travelers who are not following rules; they are energy-consuming vampires.

12. Once you are back from work, refresh and spend some time with family, take a walk, have an early dinner, and you know the sleep hygiene.

Remember, a morning routine should be tailored to your own needs and preferences. Experiment with different activities and find what works best for you to start your day feeling refreshed and ready to tackle your professional responsibilities.

Have a policy of no bath, no breakfast. No learning, no lunch. No exercise, no dinner.

The philosophy of "no learning, no lunch" reminds us that learning is a lifelong journey that should never cease. It encourages individuals to embrace a curious and open-minded approach to life, seeking opportunities for growth and deepening their understanding of the world.

This philosophy allows individuals to strive continuously for expanding knowledge, developing skills, and broadening perspectives. It acknowledges that learning is not limited to formal education but can be undertaken through reading, exploring new ideas, engaging in meaningful discussions, or seeking out new experiences.

Ultimately, the philosophy of "no learning, no lunch" underscores the belief that learning and personal growth are essential ingredients for a fulfilling and meaningful life. It encourages individuals to make learning a priority and to nourish their minds just as they nourish their bodies.

The philosophy of "treating your body like a temple" promotes the idea of valuing and caring for our bodies as sacred, deserving of respect, and proper care.

The analogy of a temple suggests that our bodies are precious and should be treated with utmost reverence, just as a temple or holy place is treated with reverence. This philosophy emphasizes the notion that our bodies house our minds, emotions, and spirits and, therefore, should be treated with care and dignity.

By adopting this philosophy, individuals are encouraged to prioritize self-care, making choices that support their physical, mental, and emotional well-being. This may include nourishing the body with nutritious food, engaging in regular exercise, getting enough rest and sleep, and taking time for relaxation and rejuvenation.

The philosophy of "treating your body like a temple" also extends beyond physical care. It underscores the importance of cultivating positive thoughts, emotions, and relationships. It encourages individuals to pay attention to their mental and emotional well-being, seeking practices and activities that promote inner peace, happiness and overall holistic health.

The conventional understanding of health typically encompasses physical well-being, both internally and externally, and sometimes extends to include mental health. However, in the broader context of the Sanskrit term "swasthya," a radically different perspective emerges. Contrary to the common notion, the concept of swasthya encapsulates a profound understanding of health, as exemplified by the sage Ashtavakra, despite his physical deformities.

Rather than being deterred or ashamed by his bodily imperfections, Ashtavakra, with eight deformities, exclaims in ecstasy, "Wonderful, wonderful am I!" This seemingly paradoxical response stems from his profound realization that, despite his physical condition, he epitomizes perfect swastha, or being established in the SELF. Ashtavakra thus offers invaluable insight into the true essence of health.

Ashtavakra's teachings are encapsulated in the Ashtavakra Gita, a revered classic of Sanskrit literature.

This text comprises a dialogue between Ashtavakra and the royal sage Janak, revolving around essential philosophical inquiries. Anchored in Advaita, the Indian philosophy of non-duality, Ashtavakra expounds on the nature of the SELF, providing transformative wisdom to Janak and subsequent readers.

The term "swasth" commonly signifies physical health, but in Sanskrit, "swastha" fundamentally conveys being established in the SELF. This interpretation expands the horizons of understanding, transcending the Greek notion of wellness as a healthy mind in a healthy body. Swastha encompasses a state beyond mere physical robustness; it represents the only true attitude toward life where one is either swastha or unwell, with no intermediate states.

Through his interactions with Ashtavakra, Janak experiences a profound transformation, becoming established in the SELF. A swastha individual is characterized by inner tranquility, having transcended the duality of opposing forces. Ashtavakra emphasizes the state of "shoonya chitta," a blank mind devoid of all pairs of opposites, akin to the stithaprajna described in the Bhagavad Gita.

The swastha person perceives the world as a projection of the SELF, residing in a state of indifference toward worldly circumstances. Ashtavakra elucidates that such an individual, dwelling in the SELF as Atmaram, experiences no afflictions and remains unaffected by physical deformities, living with a sense of wonder and contentment—always.

By treating our bodies like temples, individuals are encouraged to be mindful of the impact of their actions and choices on their bodies and overall well-being. This philosophy inspires individuals to develop a sense of deep self-respect and gratitude for the incredible gift of having a healthy and functioning body.

Ultimately, the philosophy of "treating your body like a temple" reminds us of the inherent value and importance of self-care. It encourages us to honor and respect our bodies, recognizing them as the vessels through which we experience life and navigate the world. By treating our bodies with love and care, we can strive to live harmoniously and fully in mind, body, and spirit.

7

Story Time

You can be the best in the world (BIW) only if you try to awaken your best self. There will be struggles and roadblocks. When you taste success, you will feel it's all worth it. Success is like a mango; when it's unripe and too small, it tastes bitter. When you take on a new challenge, it tastes bitter. If you accept and move on a bit and let the mango grow further, it tastes sour. You can eat it with some salt and chili powder. When you take the road less traveled and you feel good about it, and people appreciate and you are suitably rewarded for your efforts and hard work, it feels gorgeous like a ripe mango, absolutely delicious.

Unfortunately, there is no shortcut to success. Everyone I meet is asking for a 2-minute formula for success, that click of one switch, which can change their life. I call this the magic formula for success. I also call this a lottery-winning mindset. Even if you win the lottery, you will again be at the level of wealth you started with, back to square one. There is this program called *Who Wants to Be a Millionaire in India.*

It's in the Kaun language Crorepati and is hosted by the iconic Bollywood actor, Mr. Amitabh Bachchan. One contestant, Sushil Kumar, won Rs 5 Crore but failed to invest the money wisely. As a result, he lost everything and went bankrupt. In an interview, he revealed, "The worst phase of my life began after winning the show and the large sum of money. I was happier and more at peace before winning it."

On the flip side, Mr. Amitabh Bachchan had earned huge wealth by acting. He was advised to invest the money in business, and he opened his company called ABCL. However, the company went bankrupt, and Mr. Bachchan lost all his money. He had to start all over again, working tirelessly hard. Known for his punctuality, professionalism and discipline, he regained all his wealth back by acting in movies and TV shows.

Arjun says, "I understand master, there is no substitute for hard work. I will work hard. Please help me and show me the path; I shall promise to put in my 100% effort."

Yes, Arjun, now I know you need this badly. Let's walk toward the first step, passion. I will tell you a story about a passionate filmmaker. I know you love stories.

* * *

There is this passionate story of an Indian filmmaker, a stubborn perfectionist, K Asif, and I am referring to the epic movie Mughal-E-Azam, for which K Asif was the producer and director. He was in his 20s when he started the film. He was a man who never cared for money. He made a movie worth crores but lived in rented accommodation, never owned a car, and used to travel in a taxi.

Asif started the shoot of the movie in the year 1945 and had a huge star cast. In the year 1947, India got its independence, and during partition, the financier of the film went to settle in Pakistan. Chandramohan, who was *playing* Akbar, died, forcing Asif to abandon two years' worth of work.

As per the story narrated by the film's music director Naushad, Asif wanted to match the reality of Akbar's Era. Akbar ruled the Indian subcontinent from 1556 to 1605. Asif wanted to replicate the era in his film, so he brought the best tailors from Delhi. While they made the movie in Mumbai, which also has the finest artisans, he aimed for the best quality.

To make the jewelry, he got the artisans from Hyderabad. He got the best designers from Kolhapur to design the crown. He used to say, "No compromise; I want the best of the best." Tansen was the prolific singer in Akbar's court. Asif asked Naushad who could match Tansen to the current singers. Naushad said, "Bade Ghulam Ali Khan Saab can match the style of singing."

"Unfortunately, he does not sing for films; he sings only in private concerts," Asif said,

"Take me to Bade Ghulam Ali Khan Saab," Naushad said,

"What is the use? He will outrightly refuse to sing," Asif insisted, and both of them traveled to Lucknow to meet Bade Ghulam Ali Khan at his residence.

Naushad said, "He is Asif, and he is making an epic film, Mughal-E-Azam, and he wants you to sing a song in that film."

Ghulam Ali Khan refused, saying, "Naushad, you know I don't sing for films. What made you travel so far?"

Asif was a chain smoker. He lights his cigarette and says, "Bade Ghulam Ali Khan, but you will only sing the song." Bade Ghulam Ali Khan Saab got angry and took Naushad to the next room and asked him to explain what was happening. Naushad said, "Sir, he is a madman. Despite saying a hundred times that you won't sing for the films, he insisted on meeting you." Bade Ghulam Ali Khan Saab said, "If this is the matter, look how I will chase him out."

Both of them entered the meeting room. Bade Ghulam Ali Khan Saab said, "You want me to sing in this film? Fine, I will sing as a special case; however, I will charge Rs 50,000 for a song." Bade Ghulam Ali Khan Saab thought Asif would run away listening to the huge sum. In those days, singers used to charge 100 to 200 Rs per song. Asif lights his cigarette and said, "You will only and only sing this song," and reached out to his pocket and placed 10,000 rupees. He said, "I will pay the rest of the cash during recording in Mumbai, but you will and only you will sing this song."

Master said, "Arjun, once you walk toward this path, there is no looking back. Have immense faith. I will tell you a beautiful story of a miracle, man."

* * *

The most deadly battlefield in the world is Siachen. One of the most difficult deployments for the Indian Armed Forces is at Siachen because of the sub-zero temperatures, tough terrain, and an adversarial neighbor. But despite difficulties, the Indian Army had maintained its resolve, and tales of courage and bravery had emerged from the frigid heights of Siachen.

The tale of Lance Naik Hanumanthappa Koppad is one such example.

For thirteen years of his army service, Lance Naik Hanumanthappa had experience serving in a variety of operational settings under trying circumstances. Initially, from 2003 to 2006, he served in Jammu and Kashmir, actively participating in anti-terrorist operations.

He was deployed to the Siachen post in August 2015, a place known for its harsh, unforgiving conditions. When a snow avalanche roared down on the Indian Army post on February 3, 2016, Lance Naik Hanumanthappa was stationed at his post, keeping watch over the Pakistani border. A massive avalanche, buried Lance Naik Hanumanthappa and nine other Indian soldiers under 25 feet of snow.

A major rescue effort was launched by the Indian Army, but they had to search for and save Lance Naik Hanumanthappa for six days. Lance Naik Hanumanthappa miraculously survived after spending close to six days under the snow. He was airlifted to New Delhi, where the military hospital in Delhi provided his medical care.

The nation prayed for Lance Naik Hanumanthappa's recovery. However, on February 11, the brave soldier's fight for life was over. Due to multiple organ failures, he passed away.

An honorable and dedicated soldier who gave his life to the country was Lance Naik Hanumanthappa. He received the Sena Medal in recognition of his valor, dedication and heroic sacrifice.

* * *

Arjun says, "Agreed, master," with immense passion and faith. "I move ahead, tell me more. I am feeling positive." Master said, "How positive are you, Arjun?" Arjun said, "I still have the negative thoughts cropping up."

Flip your inner switch from negative to positive, Arjun.

Change ANTS is an acronym for Automatic Negative Thoughts, and APTS is an acronym for Automatic Positive Thoughts.

A few researchers claim that the thoughts per day range from 12,000 to 60,000. A few claims it to be over 70,000. But no one guarantees their research. It's a myth and let's ignore the numbers at the moment and consider it's a lot of thoughts, but we all agree that the thoughts pour over our heads like raindrops. Now, if you recollect the thoughts, there are more negative than positive thoughts because our brain always wants to protect us from unforeseen danger. From the time we humans evolved from the forests, our mammal brain has changed little. In the forest, the brain is always protecting us from danger; if something is moving, it can be lunch or you can be lunch to the moving threat. Over time, if you practice nurturing positive thoughts and shrug out the negative thorns from the garden of your mind, you will be a positive person. Below are the two techniques that shall help you develop positive thoughts.

There are two practical techniques to do so, and I have benefited from this. To a certain extent, I keep the negative thoughts at bay. I have a rubber wristband with "change" written on it. I call it a change band; I wear this on my hand, and whenever a negative thought pops in, I pull the change band. It hurts and signals the brain, saying I've got this and I am in charge of it.

I call this the ANT bite and turn the negative thoughts into a positive one, giving a strong message to the brain saying you are signaling me with a thought which might hurt, just because you produced the thought, I got hurt from the band and this pain is to be avoided. In the traffic signal, how the red sign is turned into blue, similarly when the negative thought pops in, I pull the band and send a pain signal to the brain, showing a red light, and replace the negative thought with a positive one, showing a green light to the positive thought to run over the mind. This will help a lot in controlling the negative thoughts.

The second technique is fairly simple. Take a bowl of black and white pebbles and two empty bowls. As and when a negative thought pops in, put one black pebble in the bowl. If a positive thought pops in, put a white pebble in the bowl. Initially, you will see many black pebbles and very few white pebbles. Over time and with practice, this will change, and you will have more white pebbles than black, changing most of your negative thoughts to positive and hence making you a completely positive person and your surroundings also positive.

It all boils down to mind management. If you learn the art of regulating your mind, then this is the right time to live on this planet joyously. If you continue to be a slave to your servant's servant, your mind is your servant, and your senses are your servant's servant. If you become a slave to your senses, then you will remain as a slave till you transform.

* * *

Understanding the Concept:

The idea that repeated thoughts become your reality is rooted in the principles of cognitive psychology and the law of attraction. This implies that your consistent thoughts and beliefs shape how you see things, act, and experience life.

This concept emphasizes the importance of maintaining a positive and constructive mindset to create a fulfilling and successful life.

How It Works:

1. Neural Pathways:

Our brains are incredibly adaptable and capable of forming new neural pathways based on our thoughts and experiences. When you repeatedly think about something, your brain strengthens the neural connections associated with those thoughts. Over time, these reinforced pathways make it easier for those thoughts to become automatic, influencing your behavior and decision-making processes.

2. Self-Fulfilling Prophecy:

Repeated thoughts can lead to self-fulfilling prophecies. If you constantly think positively about your abilities and potential, you are more likely to take actions that align with those beliefs, leading to positive outcomes. Conversely, negative thoughts can lead to self-doubt and hesitation, resulting in missed opportunities and negative outcomes.

3. Perception and Focus:

Your thoughts shape your perception of reality. When you focus on positive thoughts, you are more likely to notice opportunities, solutions, and positive aspects of situations.

This positive focus can lead to a more optimistic outlook and proactive behavior. On the other hand, negative thoughts can narrow your focus, making you more likely to see obstacles and challenges, which can hinder your progress.

4. Emotional Impact:

Repeated thoughts also influence your emotional state. Positive thoughts can generate feelings of happiness, confidence and motivation, while negative thoughts can lead to stress, anxiety and depression. Your emotional state, in turn, affects your actions and interactions with others, further shaping your reality.

Practical Applications:

1. Affirmations:

Use positive affirmations to reinforce constructive thoughts. Repeating affirmations like "I am capable," "I am worthy," and "I can achieve my goals" can help rewire your brain to focus on positive beliefs.

2. Visualization:

Visualize your goals and desired outcomes regularly. By imagining yourself achieving your goals, you create a mental blueprint that guides your actions and decisions toward making those goals a reality.

3. Mindfulness and Meditation:

Practice mindfulness and meditation to become aware of your thoughts and redirect negative or unproductive ones. These practices can help you cultivate a more positive and focused mindset.

4. Gratitude Journaling:

Keep a gratitude journal to reflect regularly on and appreciate the positive aspects of your life. This practice can shift your focus from what you lack to what you have, fostering a more positive outlook.

The concept that "repeated thoughts become your reality" underscores the profound impact of our mental habits on our lives. By consciously choosing to focus on positive and empowering thoughts, you can shape your perceptions, behaviors, and ultimately, your reality. Embracing this principle can lead to a more fulfilling, successful, and joyful life.

Everything starts with a thought. By shifting your thoughts, you can change your mindset. Transforming the way you speak to yourself reshapes your inner dialogue. When you adjust the mental images you visualize and the words you use, your entire reality can transform.

This highlights the profound influence of thoughts and self-talk in shaping our lives. By intentionally choosing positive and empowering thoughts, we can create a more fulfilling and optimistic life.

Indriya Nigraha (Restraint of senses): Go on a tour from senses to the soul.

The organs are the horses; the mind is the reins; the intellect is the charioteer; the soul is the rider, and this body is the chariot. The master of the household, the king, the self of man, is sitting in this chariot. If the horses are very strong and do not obey the reins, if the charioteer, the intellect, does not know how to control the horses, then this chariot will come to grief.

But if the organs, the horses are well controlled, and if the reins, the mind, are well held in the hands of the charioteer, the intellect, the chariot reaches the goal. What is meant, therefore, by mortification? Holding the reins firmly while guiding this body and mind, not letting the body do anything it likes, but keeping them both in proper control.

For instance, when a big wave of anger has come into the mind, how are we to control that? Just by raising an opposite wave. Think of love. Sometimes a mother is furious with her husband, and while in that state, the baby comes in and baby kisses the mother, the old wave dies out, and a new wave arises love for the child that suppresses the other wave. Love is apposite to anger. Similarly, when the idea of stealing comes, non-stealing should be thought of. When the idea of hatred comes, replace it with a contrary thought. Put it simply, think like a police officer at a traffic signal. When negative thoughts appear, show a stop (red signal) and replace them with a positive thought (blue signal).

While our soul is intended to govern our mind and senses, reality often shows that our physical senses dictate the actions of our mind. Consequently, the mind leads the soul astray, diverting its attention to the distractions of the external world and preoccupying it with the pursuit of worldly knowledge and material gain.

Society often promotes the idea that enhancing our intellect will benefit us both in this life and in the hereafter. However, intellect alone cannot guide us on the path toward God. It is through love and illumination that we find our way to our Eternal Home. Saints and mystics incarnate in this world to guide us in uncovering our inner reservoir of love, primarily through the practice of meditation.

By shifting our focus away from the external world during meditation and directing it toward the inner eye, the portal to our inner sanctuary, we embark on a journey to encounter the love and Light of the Divine. This communion with the divine's love strips away layers of mind, matter, and illusion that obscure our soul. Many seekers, limited by their sensory perceptions, anticipate experiencing the divine through their physical senses. However, the Supreme can only be realized through the inner eye, the gateway to the spiritual realms.

Meditation is one of the great means of controlling the rising of these waves. By meditation, you can make the mind subdue these. You can't stop it; your anger and hatred will be subdued.

If you visit any jail and ask them what led them to where they are, they will say, "I didn't do it," because it's against their very nature. When they are angry, the waves are rapid, and they take an impulsive decision, and it happens at the heat of the moment. If the waves are slow, you have a small window of opportunity to think through in a split of a second and decide to let go or take the matter into your very own hands, or replace it with a positive one and move on.

8

Brain Waves

1. Types of Brain Waves

Delta Waves (0.5-4 Hz): Delta waves are slow waves and are typically associated with deep sleep and the unconscious mind. They are also observed in certain meditative states.

Theta Waves (4-7 Hz): Theta waves are associated with relaxation, daydreaming and light sleep. They can be involved in creativity, intuition and accessing the subconscious.

Alpha Waves (8-13 Hz): Alpha waves are associated with a state of relaxed alertness. They are often present when you close your eyes and begin to relax, and they are also linked to creative thinking.

Beta Waves (14-30 Hz): Beta waves are associated with active, analytical thought, alertness, and focused concentration. They are prevalent when you are awake and engaged in cognitive tasks.

Gamma Waves (above 30 Hz): Gamma waves are associated with high-level cognitive functions, such as perception, problem-solving, and consciousness. They are involved in the binding of information from different brain areas.

2. Brain Wave Patterns:

Brain wave patterns can change depending on an individual's state of consciousness and mental activity. For example:

When you are fully awake, your brain primarily exhibits beta wave patterns, indicating active, analytical thought.

When you close your eyes and relax, you may transition to alpha wave patterns, suggesting a state of relaxation and receptivity.

In deeper states of relaxation or during meditation, theta waves may dominate, facilitating creativity and access to the subconscious.

During deep sleep, delta waves are prevalent, reflecting a state of restorative rest.

3. Clinical and Research Applications:

Brain wave patterns have various clinical and research applications. Electroencephalography (EEG) is a common method for recording brain waves and is used in diagnosing neurological conditions, studying sleep patterns, and investigating cognitive processes. For instance, EEG can be used to monitor and diagnose disorders like epilepsy, as well as to study the effects of meditation and mindfulness on brain wave patterns.

4. Mindfulness and Brain Waves:

Mindfulness practices, such as meditation and deep relaxation, have been shown to influence brain wave patterns. These practices often promote shifts from beta to alpha, or even theta waves, which are associated with states of relaxation and heightened awareness. This can be linked to the reported benefits of reduced stress, improved focus, and increased creativity associated with mindfulness.

In summary, "mind waves" are not a recognized term, but they may be synonymous with "brain waves." Brain waves represent electrical activity in the brain, categorized by frequency and associated with different states of consciousness and cognitive processes. Understanding brain waves is essential in fields such as neuroscience, psychology and meditation, as they offer insights into mental states and can be harnessed for various applications, including clinical diagnoses and research into the mind's functioning.

Arjun says, "I have tried meditation before, but could not focus." Can you please elaborate on focus and concentration, master?

Master continues, Swami Vivekananda said, "The difference between an ordinary and a great person lies in concentration." This may make you think how only focus and concentration can make an average person a great person.

* * *

We live in an era of constant distractions. Author Dandapani explains this beautifully in his book called 'Unwavering focus'. Dandapani says in our modern-day lifestyles mean that attention is continuously being stolen from us—from the endless stream of notifications on our phones, to constantly switching between tasks and tabs, and spending hours scrolling on social media. It's no wonder many of us may find it hard to concentrate.

Teachers and parents have constantly asked us to concentrate at school and home, but nobody teaches us how to concentrate. Focus is to cut down all distractions and hold on to the task at hand. This comes with practice.

If you want to concentrate on something and you have been distracted, bring your focus right back to the task. Whenever or whatever you have been distracted with, bring the focus gently and right back to the subject. With constant practice, you will focus on the task. If you keep practicing distraction throughout the day, you will be a champion at distraction. Addiction to distraction is the death of your creative production.

Focusing on the small details is indeed crucial for achieving excellence and mastery in any endeavor. Paying attention to the tiny details allows us to refine our skills, improve our work, and demonstrate a higher level of craftsmanship. It shows dedication and a commitment to excellence. Whether it's art, craftsmanship, problem-solving, or any other aspect of life, taking care of the small things can have a significant impact on the overall outcome.

Enlightenment is quite straightforward, actually. It boils down to our attention and where we focus it. Typically, our attention is consumed by the thoughts and images flitting through our minds, dwelling on memories of the past, or dreams of the future. Rarely do we focus on being fully aware of ourselves in the present moment.

Physically, we're here and now, reading these words. But mentally, our attention often drifts away from this moment, getting caught up in formulating responses based on past experiences or future projections. Even though we believe we're present, if we're not consciously self-aware in the moment, we're essentially elsewhere, dwelling in the past or future.

Failing to be present robs us of the essence of life, because life can only be lived in the here and now. True enlightenment lies in being fully aware of our existence in the present moment. It's that simple. While we can remember or imagine life, it can only be experienced in the present. As long as we cling to identities formed from the past or future, we miss out on the conscious experience of life.

This brings us to the ego — both a hindrance and a complement to enlightenment. The ego arises from the identities we create by attaching ourselves to past thoughts, feelings, sensations and actions, or projecting them into the future. But this identity, tethered to memories and projections, isn't truly alive in the present. While we defend our egos vehemently, they often keep us asleep to the present moment, even deadened to it.

Though ego serves as a tool to navigate the world and gives us a sense of existence, its ultimate purpose is higher. It's meant to teach us how to live fully aware in the present and to transform our mortal identities into something timeless and eternal.

If you consider multitasking will increase your productivity, you are completely wrong. Neuroscience consultant Marilee Springer says, "I know multitasking to slow people down by 50% and add 50% more mistakes." Multitasking is putting your brain on drugs. There is a whole body of research that shows that multitasking makes you less productive, less creative, and more likely to make a bad decision. Multitasking is like continuously changing channels of your mind. Sharpen your intellect by making it a habit to do one thing at a time. Rediscover the value of consecutive tasking instead of diluted quality that comes from multitasking. Exceptional work, which I call a masterpiece, comes with a period of deep concentration. Nothing excellent ever comes from a scattered effort.

9

Flow

Let's say the information available in front of you is like a vast buffet laid out in front of you, and your brain is a plate that can take a limited quantity from the buffet and is aware of the capacity it can hold. It draws parallels between how computers process data (in binary bits) and how the human brain processes information from the environment. Let's elaborate on this analogy:

1. Information as a Buffet:

Imagine information as a vast buffet spread out in front of you. This buffet represents all the sensory inputs and stimuli from your environment, including what you see, hear, touch, taste, and smell. This wealth of information is like a digital buffet, with an array of choices.

2. Brain as a Consumer:

In this analogy, your brain acts as the consumer at this buffet. Just like a person at a buffet table, your brain can only take in a limited amount of information at a time. The brain's capacity to process information is finite, much like the way a plate can only hold a certain amount of food.

3. Bits of Information:

The term "bits" in this analogy refers to the binary code used in computing. It's a way to represent information as either 0 or 1, which are the fundamental units of digital data. In the context of the brain, "bits" symbolize the discrete pieces of information your brain can process and understand.

4. Selective Consumption:

Much like how you select specific dishes at a buffet, your brain selectively consumes information from the environment. It focuses on certain aspects of the sensory input based on your attention, interests, and priorities. This selective consumption is similar to how you pick and choose items from the buffet that appeal to your taste.

5. Cognitive Load and Capacity:

Just as a buffet-goer can't sample everything due to the limits of their stomach's capacity, the human brain has a finite cognitive capacity. This means that it can only process a certain amount of information effectively. When the brain is overloaded with too much information, it can become overwhelmed, similar to how overloading a plate at the buffet can lead to discomfort.

6. Filtering and Prioritization:

To manage the information "buffet," your brain employs various filtering and prioritization mechanisms. These include attention, memory and cognitive biases, which help you focus on what's most relevant and important to your current goals and interests.

7. Implications for Information Consumption:

The analogy highlights the importance of mindful information consumption. Just as you make choices at the buffet to avoid overeating, it's essential to be selective in what you focus on in your environment. This can help manage cognitive load, reduce stress and improve the quality of information processing.

In summary, the analogy of the brain consuming information as "bits" from a buffet illustrates how the human brain processes external stimuli in a selective and finite manner. Recognizing the brain's capacity for information processing is important for effective information management, cognitive health and overall well-being. Just as you choose your buffet items carefully to enjoy a satisfying meal, you can choose to focus on specific information that enriches your understanding and experience.

* * *

Modern positive psychology suggests that the human brain has a limited capacity to attend to and process information at any given time. This concept is closely related to the work of Mihaly Csikszentmihalyi, a renowned psychologist known for his research on the psychology of optimal experience and the concept of "flow."

1. Limited Cognitive Capacity:

Modern positive psychology acknowledges that the human brain has finite cognitive resources. These resources are responsible for processing and attending to information, and they are not limitless. This finite capacity implies that our attention, focus, and processing abilities are constrained by the brain's capacity to handle incoming information.

2. Flow and Optimal Experience:

Mihaly Csikszentmihalyi's work on flow theory is central to understanding how the brain's limited capacity relates to positive psychology. He describes "flow" as a state of deep engagement and complete absorption in an activity. In this state, individuals often lose track of time and experience a sense of fulfillment and happiness. Achieving flow requires matching the level of challenge with one's skill set. When the challenge is too low, people become bored; when it's too high, they become anxious. Flow occurs when the challenge is just right.

3. Attentional Focus in Flow:

One of the key elements of flow is the laser-like focus of attention. When in a state of flow, individuals allocate their limited cognitive resources to the task at hand, effectively shutting out distractions and irrelevant information. This heightened focus is critical for achieving a state of flow and experiencing optimal performance and satisfaction.

4. Implications for Positive Psychology:

In the context of positive psychology, understanding the limitations of the brain's capacity for information processing has several implications:

Mindfulness and Well-Being: Mindfulness practices that involve focusing on the present moment and eliminating mental clutter can enhance well-being. By training the mind to direct its attention more effectively, individuals can improve their quality of life.

Positive Interventions: Positive psychologists use various interventions, such as gratitude journaling or savoring positive experiences, to help individuals allocate their cognitive resources to positive and meaningful aspects of life, which can improve overall life satisfaction.

Stress Reduction: Recognizing the finite nature of cognitive resources underscores the importance of stress management. Overloading the brain with excessive information and demands can lead to reduced well-being. Learning to manage stress and prioritize tasks is essential for maintaining a mental balance.

Throughout the course of our evolution, stress has remained a constant companion, manifesting in various forms. What we term as 'stress' is an intricate blend of physical and psychological reactions to challenging or intimidating stimuli. On the one hand, it propels us to enhance our efforts for survival and resilience. Without stress, we might linger in comfort zones, devoid of motivation. Conversely, stress disrupts our equilibrium, dampens our spirits, and, if mishandled, can lead to numerous physical and mental ailments.

While previous generations faced their own trials and pressures, our contemporary challenges seem more daunting. Today, we navigate noisy, polluted environments, grapple with climate shifts and natural calamities, confront political polarization, struggle with distant and fragile relationships, and inhabit workspaces demanding success at any cost.

Consequently, our bodies remain perpetually fatigued, our minds cluttered, leaving us with scant resources to combat stress. The outcome is chronic and incapacitating stress.

We often attribute this predicament to external factors and ponder over how to alter them. However, stress is primarily an internal response to external conditions, necessitating internal transformation. Most stress can be effectively managed if we grasp the roots of our discontent, modify our subjective reactions to frustrations, and rewire our perspectives.

Primarily, we must disengage from irrelevant information, tasks, and worries. With limited time, physical energy and mental capacity, it's crucial to allocate resources judiciously. Discernment is key, as not all information, tasks, or worries merit our attention or energy.

Secondly, many of us harbor a deep-seated desire to influence those close to us, believing it will enhance relationships and mutual happiness. Yet, this often leads to conflict when others resist or fail to align with our views. In such instances, acceptance of life's uncontrollable aspects is essential. Letting go of futile pursuits and focusing on personal growth fosters peace and fulfillment.

Ultimately, inner tranquility and happiness stem not from external circumstances, but from internal harmony. Embracing ease, shedding unnecessary burdens, and aligning with our inner rhythm make distressing a natural part of life.

5. Practical Application:

In practical terms, this understanding of limited cognitive capacity emphasizes the importance of mindful focus, efficient task management and the pursuit of activities that align with one's skills and interests. By optimizing the allocation of cognitive resources, individuals can enhance their well-being and achieve states of flow where they experience joy and fulfillment.

In summary, modern positive psychology, in line with Csikszentmihalyi's work, recognizes that the human brain has a finite capacity for processing information. This understanding has practical implications for promoting well-being, optimizing attention, and achieving flow states characterized by deep engagement and happiness.

* * *

10

Yoga

Let's look at what Yoga teaches us in terms of focus.

The 8 limbs of Yoga are Yama, Niyama, Asana, Pranayama, Dharana, Dhyana and Samadhi. I have covered Pranayama in the previous chapter. Dharana, Dhyana and Samadhi will be covered below. For the rest of the limbs, I may have to fight it out with my editor to give me more pages. Unfortunately, the same shall be covered in my next volume.

Dharana in Sanskrit means focused concentration. It's the sixth limb of yoga, and it refers to the act of holding and maintaining a focus on a single thing. Dha means holding or maintaining, and Ana means 'other' or something else.

Dharana is closely linked to two other limbs: the fifth limb called pratyahara, which refers to the withdrawing of the senses, and the seventh limb called dhyana, which translates to 'meditative absorption.'

Swami Vivekananda says, "as the tortoise can draw in his legs, and if you strike him, not one foot comes out, even so the sage can draw all his sense organs inside," and nothing can force them out. Nothing can shake him, no temptation or anything. Let the universe tumble about him. It does not make one ripple in his mind.

As the tortoise tucks its feet and head inside the shell, and you may kill it and break it in pieces, yet it will not come out, even so, the character of that man who has control over his motives and organs is unchangeably established. He controls his own inner forces, and nothing can draw them out against his will. Through this continuous reflex of good thoughts, good impressions moving over the surface of the mind, the tendency for doing good becomes strong, and as a result, he will control the Indriya's (the sense organs).

* * *

Arjun interrupts the master. "Master, do you mean to say, be passionate, have faith, focus, and meditate, and one shall be peaceful and blissful?"

Master says, "Humans are supposed to be peaceful and blissful living beings; however, in the quest for food and material accumulation, we become restless and unhappy."

* * *

Every morning, when you wake up, you are blissful. The alarm rings, and you need to reach out to the alarm and switch it off. The mind will say how you missed out on sleep all week. It's the weekend, and you need to sleep for some more time, and the article you read about 8-hour mandatory sleep. The conflict starts within and disturbs your peace to begin with.

Then you pick up the cell phone to check the messages. That's the worst habit. Never pick up your cell phone during the first hour in the morning. We call this the golden hour of the day. Give some time to yourself to reflect on your day. Take a walk in nature. Your brain and body need to sweat. Do Yoga, meditate, write a gratitude journal, and prepare yourself for a peaceful day, as explained in details earlier.

After an hour of nourishing your body and mind, like they say in the aircraft landing, now you are free to use the mobile phone and better prepared to answer the texts, call emails, and not the social media feed. The entire world is waiting to attack you with the arrows, such as texts, voice notes, emails and other forms. In fact, the entire world will attack us with the arrows the whole day and up till night, sometimes not letting you sleep. How do you handle the arrows?

The concept of the "second arrow of suffering" is indeed associated with Buddhism and the teachings of Gautama Buddha.

The "first arrow" of suffering in Buddhism refers to the inevitable pain and difficulties that arise in life, such as physical illness, loss or emotional distress. These sufferings are considered being a natural part of human existence.

The "second arrow" of suffering, however, is said to be self-inflicted and stems from our reaction to the initial pain or suffering. It refers to the additional suffering we experience due to our resistance, aversion, or attachment to the pain. This secondary level of suffering arises from our mental and emotional reactions, such as anger, fear, frustration, or clinging to the past.

Things magnify the suffering. Many times, the ultimate disaster we're ruminating upon hasn't even happened. We may worry, for example, that we have cancer and that we're going to die soon. We don't know, and our fear of the unknown makes the pain grow even bigger.

The second arrow may take the form of judgment ("how could I have been so stupid?"), fear ("what if the pain doesn't go away?"), or anger ("I hate that I'm in pain. I don't deserve this!"). We can quickly conjure up a hell realm of negativity in our minds that multiplies the stress of the actual event by 10 times or even more. Part of the art of suffering well is learning not to magnify our pain by getting carried away in fear, anger, and despair. We build and maintain our energy reserves to handle the big sufferings; the little sufferings, we can let go.

If you lose your job, of course, it's a normal response to feel fear and anxiety. It is true that in most cases, to be out of work is a suffering; and there is real danger attached if you don't have enough to eat or can't afford the necessary medicine. But you don't need to make this suffering worse by spinning stories in your head that are much worse than the reality.

Some people in this situation may think, "I'm no good at this or that," or "I'll never get another job," or "I failed my family." It's important to remember that everything is impermanent. Suffering can arise or work itself out for anyone at any moment. Instead of throwing good energy away on condemning yourself or obsessing over what catastrophes might be lurking around the corner, you can simply be present with the real suffering that is right in front of you, with what is happening right now.

Mindfulness is recognizing what is there in the present moment. Suffering is there, yes; but what is also there is that you are still alive: "Breathing in, I know I'm alive." Your eyes still work: "Breathing in, I'm aware of my eyes. Breathing out, I smile to my eyes." To have eyes in good condition is a wonderful thing. Because you have eyes in good condition, there's a paradise of shapes and colors available to you at every moment. There are those among us who have gone blind.

Happiness is possible immediately, even if not everything is perfect. When you look at the person you love, if he or she is absorbed in anxiety, you can help that person to get out. "Darling, do you see the sunset? Do you see the spring coming?" This is mindfulness. Mindfulness is for making us aware of what is happening now. Not only are there always conditions of happiness present in me, but they are also all around me.

If you can avoid arrows from the external world, you have won the game and remain peaceful and blissful.

* * *

Arjun says, "You mean to say if I practice the above, I will be happy?"

* * *

The happiness we have in this modern world is like building up tension and releasing it. A nice flashy car in the advertisements with models smiling. A desire pops in to buy the car. You build the tension, thinking you will also smile like the model. You work hard and take loans and buy the car, for a short while, smiling, then again the happiness is gone. Meanwhile, if there is a small scratch or dent, it leads to unhappiness almost immediately. Let me build up one more tension. All the money and energy spent in trying to be happy. Where is the result? Not there. The delightful taste of the food, wonderful fragrances of flowers you smelled, wonderful movies and other beautiful sights you have seen. Vague memories faded away, very fine traces of it have been left. Want to spend your rest of your life like that?

Can humans ever be perfect, or are we naturally flawed? Society expects flawless performance from us, yet achieving greatness often feels like an impossible task. Our ancestors aimed for perfection and sometimes reached it. In just nineteen verses, Chapter two of the Gita explains what perfection is and shows us how to reach it.

So, what is excellence? What stops us from reaching our goals? Desire gets in the way of what we want, leaving us feeling dissatisfied and stuck. Chasing after what we desire often leaves us disappointed, while letting go of those desires brings satisfaction.

Everyone wants to be happy, but not many know how to find it. The Bhagavad Gita has the answer.

Happiness comes from how many desires we fulfill compared to how many we have. By either fulfilling more desires or wanting less, we can become happier. However, running after desires usually makes us less happy over time.

Imagine needing just a headphone but getting distracted by a watch and a smartphone in the Amazon app with heavy discounts. Even though you get the glasses, you end up wanting more things, which makes you less happy and the discounts you missed. But if you focus on wanting less, your happiness can grow a lot. Eventually, if you have no desires at all, you can be infinitely happy.

Desire comes from feeling empty inside, like being hungry when your stomach is empty. Even after getting what we want, that empty feeling sticks around because it's not real. We're actually full inside, but we don't realize it.

We don't really need things from the world; we need to understand how full we already are. Like a child who doesn't know they're from a rich family, we need to realize our true value to change our lives.

We're not just rich; we're infinitely rich. By wanting better things, we can feel more joy. When we move from wanting simple things to wanting bigger ideas and spiritual growth, we can be infinitely happy and free from worries. This is the way to be perfect.

If you are only seeking sense pleasure, one day when you gain knowledge, you will say, "By the servant of my servant, I have been made a servant." Who is your servant? The mind. Who are the servants of the mind? The senses. I have been made a servant to the senses. The eyes say, "See this," you will see this; your tongue says, "Eat this," you eat that; your skin says, "Touch that," you touch that, despite knowing it's not good for you. Freedom from this servitude will give you great peace. Try it and see. Try it for one day and compare it to the other days, and see which is better.

Whether you tend to think about what brings you happiness, it's worth considering the chemistry behind our moods, emotions, and overall well-being.

* * *

There are four key hormones that influence our feelings of happiness. Firstly, **dopamine**, often called the feel good hormone, is released in our brains when we achieve goals or experience pleasure. However, relying too much on dopamine rushes can lead to addictive behaviors.

Secondly, **serotonin**, a mood-regulating hormone, plays a role in enhancing our mood, optimism, and sleep quality. It's interesting to note that most serotonin is produced in our gut, emphasizing the importance of a healthy diet and lifestyle.

Social comparisons and excessive stress can affect serotonin levels, highlighting the significance of managing social interactions and stress levels.

Next, **oxytocin**, known as the love hormone, promotes feelings of safety, belonging, trust, and empathy. It's boosted through acts of love, physical touch, intimacy, and kindness toward others.

Lastly, **endorphins** act as natural pain relievers, reducing pain and stress while inducing a sense of well-being. Activities like exercise, laughter, art and meditation support the release of endorphins.

These hormones offer valuable insights into maintaining mental and emotional balance. Practicing moderation, engaging in regular exercise, spending time outdoors, maintaining a nutritious diet, fostering personal relationships, practicing gratitude, and pursuing interests are all essential for promoting overall happiness and well-being. Laughing more and not taking ourselves too seriously can also contribute to a happier life.

11

Happiness

You may ask, what is real and lasting happiness?

There are three types of blissful nature: Vishayaanadha, Bhajananda and Bhramanda. Vishayaanadha is the lowest, and Bhrahmanada is the highest.

In Sanskrit, "Vishayaananda" can be broken down into two parts: "Vishaya," meaning sense objects or worldly pleasures, and "Ananda," meaning bliss or joy. Together, "Vishayaananda" can be understood as the state of experiencing bliss by indulging in or enjoying sensory pleasures.

However, in spiritual teachings, "Vishayaananda" is often contrasted with "Bhajananda," or the bliss derived from devotional singing or worship. While Vishayaananda pertains to temporary and sensory pleasures, Bhajananda focuses on the spiritual and transcendental joy derived from connecting with the divine.

In spiritual practices and teachings, the emphasis is often on transcending Vishayaananda and seeking the deeper and lasting joy of Bhajananda, as it is believed to bring about true happiness and fulfillment.

Bhajananda is a Sanskrit term that can be broken down into two parts: "bhajana" meaning devotional singing or worship, and "ananda" meaning bliss or joy. Together, "Bhajananda" signifies the state of experiencing bliss through devotional singing or worship.

In the context of Indian music, bhajans are devotional songs typically sung in praise of a deity or spiritual figure. Bhajans can be found in various forms and styles across different regions of India. They often incorporate religious teachings, stories and messages of love, devotion, and surrender.

Participating in bhajan singing or listening to bhajans is considered a form of spiritual practice as it allows individuals to connect with the divine and experience a sense of peace, joy, and transcendence. Bhajans are often accompanied by traditional Indian musical instruments, such as harmonium, tabla, dholak, and tambura.

The practice of Bhajananda, or experiencing bliss through devotional singing, is cherished by many individuals as a way to deepen their spiritual connection and experience a sense of oneness with the divine.

The term "Brahmananda" can be understood as the state of bliss that arises from experiencing or realizing the ultimate reality, or Brahman.

The term "Brahman" refers to the ultimate reality, the absolute or the universal consciousness that underlies and encompasses all existence. It is considered being the highest truth in Hindu philosophy.

"Ananda" means bliss or joy. So, when combined, "Brahmananda" represents the bliss that arises from realizing the oneness with Brahman or the ultimate reality. It refers to a state of profound happiness, contentment, and spiritual fulfillment that transcends the temporary pleasures of the world.

In spiritual teachings and practices, the aim is often to attain Brahmananda by expanding one's consciousness, realizing the true nature of oneself and the universe, and merging with the ultimate reality. It is believed that experiencing Brahmananda leads to liberation or moksha, which is the ultimate goal of many spiritual seekers.

* * *

Master said, "I let go of my exalted reputation, my princely position, and the endless availability of sensual pleasure. But now people come to me, plead with me, and ask me to bless them with the very things I have renounced. They ask for lots of money, power, or for their children to have good grades on their exams. You are different; you asked for peace and bliss, and I knew you wanted it badly."

Arjun said, "If I tell you honestly, master, I am feeling positive, passionate toward life, and having immense faith in myself. Thank you for instilling these in me. I am very grateful to you. However, to be honest, the bliss that you promised looks like a distant dream. I want to be blissful like my boss; he has got everything, and he looks like a happy man."

Master said, "God has given you the greatest gift called life, neatly gift-wrapped. You are stuck with the wrapper. Complain about your wrapper color with your boss."

This world is called illusory because everything here is both illusion and the supreme soul.

The above statement delves into a philosophical perspective that reflects ideas found in various spiritual and philosophical traditions, particularly in Hinduism and Advaita Vedanta. Let's break down the concept:

1. The Illusory Nature of the World:

The term "illusory" implies that the material world we perceive is not as real or permanent as it seems. It's a concept that suggests that our perception of the physical world is deceptive and it can be temporary or misleading. This concept is in line with the understanding that the external world is subject to change, impermanence, and transience.

2. Everything Is Both Illusion and the Supreme Soul:

This part of the statement introduces a key aspect of non-dualistic philosophy, where everything in the world is perceived as having two facets: illusion and the supreme soul. This duality represents a paradoxical view of reality, often associated with the Advaita Vedanta philosophy.

Illusion: In this context, the "illusion" aspect refers to the material and transient nature of the world. It suggests that the physical world is a projection or a temporary manifestation, and it is not the ultimate or absolute reality. This perspective views the world as ever-changing, impermanent, and deceptive, in that it can mislead us into believing it is the only reality.

Supreme Soul: On the other hand, the "supreme soul" aspect points to the belief in an underlying, unchanging, and eternal reality that is often referred to as the supreme soul, the ultimate truth or the absolute. In Advaita Vedanta, this supreme reality is often equated with Brahman, the universal consciousness or divine essence. It is considered the unchanging, all-pervading, and transcendent reality that underlies and connects everything in the universe.

3. Non-Dualistic Perspective:

This statement is rooted in non-dualistic philosophy, which asserts that the apparent duality in the world is an illusion and the ultimate reality is non-dual or one. In this view, the separation between the individual self (Atman) and the supreme reality (Brahman) is considered illusory. The realization of this non-dual nature is a central theme in many Eastern philosophical and spiritual traditions.

4. Implications:

The concept implies that the world, with its ever-changing and temporary nature, is ultimately unreal in comparison to the unchanging and eternal nature of the supreme soul or reality. Thus, from this philosophical standpoint, understanding and transcending the illusory nature of the world can lead to spiritual awakening and liberation (moksha), as individuals recognize their oneness with the supreme soul.

In conclusion, the statement reflects a non-dualistic perspective that considers the world as illusory due to its transient and deceptive nature, while also recognizing the supreme soul or ultimate reality as the unchanging and eternal essence that underlies everything. It is a profound philosophical concept that has influenced many spiritual and philosophical traditions, emphasizing the importance of realizing the unity of all existence.

Master said, "Listen to this story, Arjun."

12

A Bird's Flight

Once, a young girl full of hope and ambition visited me at the ashram. She came often to seek my blessings. Her parents were hardworking farmers who sent her to the city for a better education and future. Driven by determination and passion, she excelled in her studies and achieved remarkable grades. Her success caught the attention of a big corporation. Overjoyed, she was hired and given a prestigious job.

Proud and excited, she visited the ashram again to share her achievements. She described how a simple girl from a small town made her way into the corporate world.

Months passed, and the ashram noticed her absence. Her visits became rare, and I assumed her busy schedule kept her away. After a year, she returned, seeking my blessings for what she thought would be the last time.

Intrigued, I asked if she was planning to move abroad. She shook her head. Perplexed, I asked if she intended to return to her hometown. Again, she said no.

Overwhelmed by emotions, she burst into tears and revealed her struggles since joining the corporate world. Banks and creditors offered her easy loans and credit cards. Wanting to appear sophisticated, she indulged in shopping sprees and expensive salon treatments to impress her coworkers.

Soon, she found herself praised by colleagues but trapped in debt. Desperate, she saw no way out and felt life was unfair, leaving her hopeless.

Listening with compassion, I compared her situation to that of a silkworm. The silkworm spins its cocoon and feels trapped inside. Similarly, she bought fancy things to impress others and got trapped in debt.

Determined to help, I introduced her to a resourceful businessman. He restructured her loans and had some debt waived. He taught her the importance of managing finances and planning for the future.

Months later, she learned her lessons the hard way. Slowly, she cleared her debts and regained control of her life. She emerged stronger, understanding financial independence and a balanced lifestyle.

* * *

Once upon a time, in a peaceful forest, there was a bird that had managed to find a delicious piece of meat. The bird had never tasted anything so scrumptious before and it held onto it tightly, unwilling to share or let it go.

Word traveled quickly among the other birds in the forest about the bird's newfound treasure. Curiosity sparked, and soon a group of hungry birds began to gather around, hoping to get a taste of the meat for themselves.

The bird, feeling threatened by the other birds circling around, decided to take flight and find a safe place to enjoy its meal. However, to its surprise, the other birds started to chase after it, determined to get a piece of the meat.

As the chase continued, the bird grew overwhelmed and exhausted. It realized that holding onto the meat was causing more harm than pleasure. It could no longer savor the taste or appreciate the beauty of the forest, as it was constantly on the run.

Finding a moment of clarity amidst the chaos, the bird made a bold decision. It flew toward a nearby tree and, with one swift motion, dropped the meat to the forest floor.

The other birds, seeing the meat lying on the ground, quickly stopped their pursuit. With a mix of disappointment and confusion, they pecked at the abandoned meat, each taking a small share for themselves.

Once they had their fill, the other birds dispersed, leaving the bird who had originally found the meat alone. However, instead of feeling regret or longing, it felt an incredible sense of relief and freedom.

Without the weighted burden of the meat, the bird's wings felt lighter, and it could fly higher and glide effortlessly through the treetops. It now realized that holding onto something so tightly had hindered its ability to truly enjoy and experience the wonders of the forest.

Arjun, "Why do you not discern the simple fact that actually, the entire life of a human being lies within, not without? Whatever is worth gaining or losing also lies within him. On the outside, neither riches nor renunciation is worth attaining; for everything that exists outside is simply an illusion. Even heaven and hell do not exist outside. The mindset you are presently dwelling in is verily your hell. And I sincerely want to help you overcome your misery and instantly anchor you in supreme bliss."

"Let go," Arjun. "Let go of the ego, jealousy, hatred, illusion, delusions, confusion, dullness, attachment and aversion. Hold on to the feet of the lord and become one with it. This is the secret of blissfulness."

* * *

By now, the food service started on the aircraft, and the air hostess accidentally serves non-vegetarian food to the master and vegetarian food to Arjun. Arjun furiously looks at the hostess. The master gently tells her to replace his meal. Arjun asks the master, "Are you vegetarian by birth, or did you turn vegetarian after becoming a monk?" and discusses the importance of diet and health in one's life.

Master said, "I used to love non-vegetarian food. I just read a line in the Bhagavad Gita which said, 'Na himsat sarva bhutani.' It changed my world."

"Na himsat sarva bhurani" is a Sanskrit phrase that translates to "do not harm all beings." It is a principle rooted in compassion and non-violence, emphasizing the importance of treating all living beings with kindness and respect.

This concept is deeply ingrained in various religious and spiritual traditions, such as Hinduism, Buddhism, and Jainism. It promotes the idea of minimizing harm, both physical and emotional, toward all sentient beings.

By adhering to this principle, individuals are encouraged to cultivate empathy and consider the consequences of their actions on others. It extends beyond human beings and includes animals, plants and the environment as well.

Practicing "na himsat sarva bhurani" involves adopting a lifestyle that minimizes harm to all beings. It may involve following a vegetarian or vegan diet, avoiding the exploitation of animals for personal gain, promoting environmental sustainability, and treating others with kindness and compassion.

The principle of "na himsat sarva bhurani" encourages individuals to live in harmony with all beings, fostering a sense of interconnectedness and promoting a more compassionate and peaceful world.

* * *

Arjun says, "Master, but even fruits and vegetables have life. You are harming them."

Master smiled and said, "If you look at a fruit or vegetable, for example, take tomatoes. When it is raw, you need energy to pluck a raw tomato, but when it's ripe, you just have to touch it; it will fall on your lap. That's not the case with chicken or fish. Nature is always trying to communicate with you. You need to catch it; I meant the tomatoes, mangoes, apples and oranges. You have your food preference sitting next to me. I don't mind. I respect your choices and eating habits.

Arjun says, "Thank you, Master, for respecting my choice."

The Master replies, "By the end of this journey, if you like my talk, you will feel inspired and want to teach it to others."

Arjun responds, "Yes, Master, my wife needs this more than I do."

The Master advises, "Remember three important things: First, don't start your discourse until someone asks for it. Second, respect and love your listeners, and never think you are superior to them. Third, transform yourself so that people ask you how you do it. Your actions will inspire others and attract them to a transformed life." Arjun nods his head in agreement.

Arjun calls the air hostess and asks her to change the meal to the vegetarian. "You have enlightened me, master. From this moment, I turn vegetarian."

The master said, "I love your name. The name *Arjuna* is derived from the Sanskrit word *Arjuna*, which means 'white' or 'silver.' It symbolizes purity and brilliance. Arjuna is known for his exceptional archery skills, valor, and righteousness. Very upright and honest, the best student as well."

Arjun says, "Master, I have diabetes, but still I cannot resist the temptation of sweets and desserts. I believe this is one of my weaknesses. How does one overcome this? Since childhood, I like sweets."

Master says, "The Stanford marshmallow experiment,"

* * *

It was a study on delayed gratification in 1972 led by psychologist Walter Michel, a professor at Stanford University. In this study, a child aged five was offered a choice between one small but immediate reward or two small rewards if they waited for a certain period. The marshmallows were placed in front of the toddlers with clear instructions to wait for a certain period and they would be rewarded with two marshmallows; the entire activity was video recorded.

The very moment the instructor left, a few kids grabbed the marshmallows and started eating. Few kids took the instructions seriously and waited for the instructor to return to grab the incentives. The strategy they used while waiting was to look elsewhere instead of at the marshmallows. Looking at the marshmallows would tempt them to grab one.

After twenty years, Walter Michel tracked down the kids, now adults, to check how they were faring in life. To Walter Michel's surprise, the kids who waited and got two marshmallows fared well in life with good academics, jobs and careers, whereas the kids who couldn't resist the temptation and grabbed the marshmallows were having difficulties in coping with life; some were addicted to drugs, some dropped out of college, and some had criminal records.

The video was recreated and put on YouTube by someone. You can go and check the same with a title called "marshmallow experiment." I had gone to my friend's place for dinner, and they had two kids. I was sharing this story, and immediately my friend's wife wanted to experiment this with the kids. They did not have marshmallows; instead, they wanted to try with Mysore pak (a local delicacy made with sugar and flour). I asked the couple to hold on and said first to have this tested on yourself, then you can test on the kids.

They were taken aback and asked me how to test this for adults. I said next time when the iPhone gets released, can you hold your temptation and not rush to the store at midnight, stand in line, and post selfies with an iPhone, and instead wait for some time. Next time, can you not go to a movie of your favorite star on the first day, first show, instead wait for the reviews and see if the movie is worth your time?

Delayed gratification is the ability to delay an impulse for an immediate reward to receive a more favorable reward at a later time. Studies have shown that the ability to delay reward is present in highly successful people. How does one delay the impulse and hold on for a certain amount of time? Don't look at the marshmallow.

Keep your attention focused on something you love or care. Practice, practice and practice. When you have the urge, hold on to your temptation for a minute, then try five minutes, then ten minutes. After a certain period, you will master the art and consume your favorite chocolate cookie which is lying on the table whenever you desire to eat, or you may outrightly ask someone to take it off the table since you are on a sugar-free diet. This will lead to self-control, make you more confident and successful.

* * *

Arjun says, "Master, you are being kind to me, but I am getting attracted to the air hostess. Not for her service. I get enslaved to her looks. Please tell me how to overcome this weakness as well."

Master said, "Great sages and kings have felt these weaknesses."

The Shreemad Bhagavatam relates a story that perfectly illustrates this statement. The story is beautifully recited by Swami Mukundananda in his book Bhagavad Gita. You can also find this on YouTube; I just love his rendition.

13

Saubhari

Saubhari was a great sage in ancient times. He is mentioned in the Rig Veda, where there is a mantra called Saubhari Sutra. So he was no ordinary sage. Saubhari had attained such control over his body that he used to submerge himself in the river Yamuna and meditate underwater. One day, he saw two fish mating. This sight carried away his mind and senses, and the desire for sexual consummation arose in him. He abandoned his spiritual practice and came out of the water, wondering how to fulfill the desire.

At that time, the king of Ayodhya was Mandhata, who was a very illustrious and noble ruler. He had fifty daughters. Each is more beautiful than the other. Saubhari approached the king and asked for the hand of one of the fifty princesses.

King Mandhata wondered about the sanity of the sage and thought to himself, "An old man wanting to get married!" The king knew Saubhari to be a powerful sage and feared the sage might curse him if he refused. But if he consented, the life of his daughters would be ruined. He was in a dilemma. So, he said, "O holy one! I have no objection to you, and whosoever chooses you will become yours in marriage." The king was confident that none of his daughters would choose the old ascetic, and in this way, it would save him from the sage's curse.

Understanding the king's intention, Saubhari told the king that he would return the following day. That evening, he used his yogic powers to turn himself into a handsome young man. When he presented himself at the palace the next day, all the fifty princesses chose him as their husband. The king was bound by his word he had given and was compelled to marry all his fifty daughters to the sage.

Now, the king was concerned about the fights that would take place among the fifty sisters, since they would have to share a husband. However, Saubhari again used his yogic powers. Putting the king's apprehension to rest, he assumed fifty forms and created fifty palaces for his wives, and lived separately with each one of them. In this manner, thousands of years passed by. The puranas state Saubhari had many children from each of them, and those children had further children until a tiny city has been created.

One day, Saubhari came to his senses and exclaimed, *aho imam pashyata me vinasham* (Bhagavatam 9.6.50), "O Humans! Those of you who make plans to attain happiness through material acquisitions, be careful. Look at my degradation - where I was and where I am now. I created fifty bodies by my yogic powers and lived with fifty women for thousands of years. And yet, the senses did not experience fulfillment; they only kept hankering for more. Learn from my downfall and be warned not to venture in this direction."

Arjun asks, "If I truly surrender to the God with complete devotion, my winnability in life is guaranteed. I don't have to do much, and the majority of work will be done by God for me?" Master says, "No, Arjun, he will create a winning atmosphere. You need to work toward it. Let me tell you a short story.

"In the epic Mahabharata, the killing of Jayadratha is a significant event that takes place during the Kurukshetra War. Jayadratha was the son-in-law of King Dhritarashtra, who was supporting the Kauravas in the war against the Pandavas.

"During the war, Jayadratha is responsible for a significant incident known as the 'Abhimanyu Vadh', or the killing of Abhimanyu. Abhimanyu was the son of Arjuna, one of the Pandava princes, and his wife, Subhadra. He was born with exceptional skills and was trained in various forms of warfare from a young age.

"During the Kurukshetra War, Abhimanyu played a crucial role in the Pandava army. He possessed the knowledge of how to penetrate the Chakravyuha, a formation of soldiers arranged in a complex labyrinthine pattern. This knowledge was imparted to him by his father, but he was only taught how to enter the formation, not how to get out.

"On the 13th day of the war, the Kauravas, led by their best warriors, devised a strategy to trap the Pandavas in the Chakravyuha and focus their attack on Abhimanyu. They knew that once Abhimanyu entered the formation, he would be isolated from support and left vulnerable.

"Abhimanyu fearlessly charged into the Chakravyuha, breaking through the enemy lines. However, as the Pandavas were unable to follow him, he found himself alone inside the formation.

"Inside the Chakravyuha, Abhimanyu displayed his exceptional combat skills, fighting valiantly against numerous Kaurava warriors. He defeated several prominent warriors, including Dronacharya's son, Ashwatthama, Karna's son, Vrishasena, and Duryodhana's brother, Dushasana.

"However, even with his extraordinary abilities, Abhimanyu could not find his way out of the Chakravyuha. The Kaurava warriors surrounded and attacked him simultaneously. They violated the rules of warfare by attacking Abhimanyu simultaneously, which was dishonorable. Jayadratha played a significant role in preventing the Pandavas from entering the Chakravyuh formation. He also kicked the dead Abhimanyu.

"When Arjuna learns about Abhimanyu's death, he becomes consumed with grief and swears to kill Jayadratha before sunset the next day, or vows to give up his life by jumping into the fire pit. It's called agnisnan. Hearing this, Kauravas rejoiced, and the Pandavas were unhappy. The Kauravas thought Arjuna was the main warrior. If we hide Jayadratha for one day, Arjuna is gone, and the war is over. The Pandavas thought, why did Arjuna make this vow? They will hide Jayadratha tomorrow, and it will be the end of the road for us.

"Next day, as per their strategy, the Pandavas hid Jayadratha and kept Arjuna occupied. Arjuna and Krishna were searching for Jaydratha but could not find him. Time was passing quickly, and Arjuna was losing time and hope. It almost looked dark and seemed like a sunset.

"Jayadratha rejoiced and asked his warrior to check if the Sun had set. The warriors confirmed, saying it looks dark and the birds are returning to the nest; the Sun had set. Jaydratha jumps for joy and heads toward the firepit to see Arjun die, where all the Kauravas assembled. It was an eventful activity. Duryodhana invites Arjun and asks him if he remembers the vow. Arjun accepts God's wish and walks toward the firepit.

Suddenly, Shakuni enters and asks Krishna why his Sudarshan Chakra is covering the Sun. Krishna, with a smile, recalls his Sudarshana Chakra; it was broad daylight. Arjun looks at Krishna. Krishna says, "What are you looking at me for? Jaydrath is right in front of you. Pick up your bow (Ghandiv) and kill him." Jaydrath pleads with Arjun not to kill him.

Jayadratha's head is taken with the arrow far from the battlefield, finally landing on the lap of his father, Vridhakshatra. His father had been granted a boon that whoever would be responsible for his son's severed head falling onto the ground would have his own head burst into a hundred pieces. Vridhakshatra's head shatters into a hundred pieces, and both father and son get killed.

Arjun looks at Krishna and says, "What did you do?"

Krishna said, "I create winning moments."

Krishna, understanding the importance of Arjuna's oath, manipulates the positions of the Sun and creates an artificial solar eclipse known as the '*Jayadratha Vadha Parva*'.

* * *

As soon as the master finished narrating this story, there is turbulence felt and Arjun looks outside and sees that the aircraft engine is on fire.

Arjun screams, "Master, look out the window. The engine is on fire." Very soon the smoke is felt in the cabin.

Arjun says, "Master, we are going to die."

The master calmly says, "I think there are two engines. If one failed or is on fire, we have the second one, right?"

Arjun says, "Yes, master, I think you are right and we will be safe."

Pilot makes an announcement about the engine catching fire, and the second engine is not reacting. There is an emergency, and he is doing his best. Hearing this, Arjun started weeping profusely. "My parents, my wife, what will happen to my child if I die?"

Master calmly responds, "You don't have to worry about your job, the important sale, the layoff and the party, right?"

Arjun says, "Master, I am not interested in this talk anymore. Leave me alone. I want to die peacefully. How can you be so fearless about the death?"

* * *

The universal truth is that death is an inevitable part of life, yet it often catches us off guard despite our awareness of its certainty. Yama, a figure from Hindu mythology, is portrayed as the Lord of Death, responsible for determining the fate of souls after death. The metaphorical use of Yama in the statement highlights the sudden and unexpected nature of death, which can come for anyone at any time.

Despite our intellectual understanding of death's inevitability, many of us tend to live our lives as if it is something distant or abstract, something that happens to others but not to ourselves. We might even push the thought of death to the back of our minds, avoiding contemplation of our mortality. This tendency to deny or ignore the reality of death leaves us unprepared for its eventual arrival.

When death does come, it disregards age, wealth, status or any other worldly distinction. It is the great equalizer, affecting everyone indiscriminately. This aspect of death's impartiality is highlighted by the phrase "spares no one."

In essence, the statement serves as a reminder of the importance of acknowledging and accepting the inevitability of death. By embracing this reality, we can live more fully and purposefully, making the most of our time and relationships while we have them. It urges us to prioritize what truly matters in life and to approach each moment with mindfulness and gratitude, knowing that our time is finite.

The life is given by the God. In case if he wishes to take it back, make his job easy by surrendering to his feet and thanking him for whatever he has given in this life. Don't worry, Arjun. Whatever you possess in this life is nothing compared to what is in store for you in the higher abodes.

One unnecessary suffering that we can let go of is the suffering of fear. So many of us walk around with the pain and agitation of useless fear, whether that is the fear of dying, fear of hunger, injury or loss, fear of what might happen if we do the wrong thing, or fear of being hurt by or of hurting someone we care about.

Many people suffer due to the fear of dying. We want to live forever. We fear annihilation. We don't want to pass from being into nonbeing. This is understandable. If you believe that one day you will cease to exist altogether, it can be very scary. But if you take the time to still the activities of body and mind and look deeply, you may see that you are dying right at this very moment. You think that you will die in a few years, or 20 years, or 30 years. That's not true. You are dying now.

You have been dying all the time. It's actually very pleasant to die, which is also to live. There are many cells inside your body that are dying as you read these words. Fifty to 70 billion cells die each day in the average human adult. You are too busy to organize funerals for all of them! At the very same time, new cells are being born, and you don't have the time to sing Happy Birthday to them. If old cells don't die, there's no chance for new cells to be born. So death is a very good thing. It's very crucial for birth.

You are undergoing birth and death at this very moment. While most people are intensely afraid of dying, there are also people who are weary of living. They get bored after 50, 70, or maybe only 20 or 30 years. They find life unbearable and are seeking nonbeing. Some of them think that suicide is a way to end the suffering and to pass from the realm of being into nonbeing. Both of these preconceptions cause suffering because they ignore the reality that life and death always go together.

You can't take one out of the other. Even after your so-called death, you will continue in some way. Deep looking can dismantle these kinds of notions. There is no birth and death; everything dies and renews itself all the time. When you get that kind of insight, you no longer tire yourself out with anxiety and aversion.

According to Hindu tradition, sesame seeds (til) and water hold significant symbolic meaning after the death of a person. These rituals are a part of the last rites and are believed to be essential for the departed soul's journey to the afterlife.

* * *

Sesame seeds: Sesame seeds are considered auspicious and are associated with purification and the removal of impurities. In Hindu rituals, offering sesame seeds during funerals is believed to help cleanse the departed soul of any sins or impurities it may have accumulated during its lifetime. These seeds are often offered in the form of a tarpan or pindam, which is a small ball of rice mixed with sesame seeds and offered to the departed soul during the rituals. The belief is that by offering sesame seeds, the soul can achieve liberation (moksha) and find peace in the afterlife.

Water: Water is considered a purifier and plays a significant role in Hindu rituals. After the death of a person, water is poured into the mouth of the deceased during the final rites. This act is believed to quench the thirst of the departed soul and provide comfort during their journey to the next realm. Water is also used for cleansing and purifying the body before cremation or burial.

* * *

Both sesame seeds and water symbolize purification and liberation in Hindu funeral customs. They are offered with the intention of helping the departed soul find peace, cleanse any sins or impurities, and aid in their transition to the afterlife. These rituals hold spiritual significance and are performed with reverence and respect for the deceased.

In addition to the symbolic meaning of purification and liberation, sesame seeds also represent the notion that material possessions and worldly achievements are insignificant in comparison to the higher spiritual realms. They serve as a reminder that the soul's journey continues beyond this physical life and that there are greater spiritual aspirations and goals awaiting in the afterlife. It is believed that by offering sesame seeds, individuals recognize the transient nature of worldly attachments and focus on attaining spiritual growth and enlightenment.

Arjun says, "Master, it feels like I am dead now. If I look outside, I am en route to heaven or hell. I don't want to die. I will be the best version of myself and follow all your advice. Please help me. I know you have special power."

Master says, "You have a long way to go. I liked the way you said I am en route to heaven, then took a pause and said maybe hell; you are very ambitious even after death. I don't have sesame seeds, have some water to purify."

Arjun asks, "Master, what needs to be done to avoid hell and embrace heaven?"

The master said, "You need to wear a gold chain and tiara; you will be welcomed in heaven. If you wear metal handcuffs, you will be welcomed in hell, and it will continue until your next birth."

14

The Law of Karma

It is a fundamental principle in many Eastern philosophies and religions, particularly in Hinduism, Buddhism and Jainism, is the idea that your actions have consequences, and the quality of those consequences is determined by the nature of your deeds. Let's define and elaborate on the Law of Karma and how it relates to your metaphor:

Definition of the Law of Karma:

The Law of Karma is a belief that every action, whether physical, mental, or emotional, has consequences. These consequences can be experienced in this life or carried forward into future lives, depending on the belief system. The key principles of the Law of Karma include:

Cause and Effect: Karma is essentially the law of cause and effect. It suggests that every action (the cause) generates a result or consequence (the effect).

Moral Responsibility: Karma is inherently tied to moral responsibility. Good actions yield positive results, while bad actions yield negative results.

Karma Yoga is one of the four main paths of yoga in Hindu philosophy, the others being Bhakti Yoga (the path of devotion), Jnana Yoga (the path of knowledge), and Raja Yoga (the path of meditation). Karma Yoga, also known as the path of selfless action, is a spiritual practice that emphasizes performing one's duties and actions without attachment to the results. It's about using everyday actions as a means of spiritual growth and self-realization.

Here are key principles and aspects of Karma Yoga:

Selfless Action: Karma Yoga involves selflessly performing one's duties and actions without any expectation of personal gain, recognition, or reward. The focus is on the act itself, not the fruits or outcomes.

Duty and Dharma: Central to Karma Yoga is the concept of "dharma," which refers to one's duty, righteousness, or moral and ethical responsibilities. Practitioners of Karma Yoga identify their dharma in various roles, such as a parent, a teacher, a worker, etc., and perform those roles with dedication.

Detachment: Practitioners are encouraged to act with detachment from the results of their actions. This means not being overly affected by success or failure, and understanding that the outcomes are beyond their control.

Surrender: Karma Yogis often surrender the outcomes of their deeds to a higher power or the divine, recognizing that a larger cosmic order governs the universe. This surrender is an essential aspect of the practice.

Spiritual Growth: By acting selflessly and with a sense of duty, individuals on the path of Karma Yoga aim to purify their minds, transcend their ego, and progress spiritually. The ultimate goal is to realize their true nature or inner divinity.

Equality of All Actions: In Karma Yoga, no action is considered superior or inferior in a spiritual sense. Whether you are a teacher, a laborer or a leader, the key is to perform your duties with sincerity, dedication, and selflessness.

Meditation in Action: Karma Yoga can be seen as a form of meditation in action. By performing actions mindfully and with a sense of devotion, individuals can maintain a state of meditative awareness throughout their daily lives.

Service and Compassion: The practice of Karma Yoga often leads individuals to serve others and act with compassion. It encourages acts of kindness, generosity, and service to those in need.

Attitude and Intention: Your attitude and intention matter in Karma Yoga. Performing actions with a pure heart, love, and a sense of duty is more important than the external appearance of the action.

Liberation: The ultimate goal of Karma Yoga is spiritual liberation (moksha or nirvana), which is the release from the cycle of reincarnation (samsara) and the realization of one's oneness with the divine.

Examples of Karma Yoga can be found in everyday life. For instance, a nurse who cares for patients with compassion and dedication, a teacher who educates students with selflessness, or a parent who raises their children with love and responsibility, can all be considered practitioners of Karma Yoga. It's a path that underscores that spirituality can be woven into the fabric of daily life through the simple act of selfless service and performing one's duties with devotion and mindfulness.

Good karma and bad karma are central concepts in Hinduism, Buddhism, and other Indian religions, which are often collectively referred to as "karma traditions." These concepts revolve around the idea that our actions have consequences, and these consequences can affect our future experiences and circumstances.

Karma is the law of cause and effect, and it operates on the principle that every action generates a corresponding reaction.

Good Karma: Good karma, also known as "Punya" in Sanskrit, refers to the positive and virtuous actions or deeds that result in beneficial consequences. When you perform actions with good intentions, selflessness, and moral righteousness, you accumulate good karma. Here are some key points about good karma:

Positive Outcomes: Good karma tends to bring positive results and favorable experiences into one's life. This can manifest as happiness, success, good health, and harmonious relationships.

Acts of kindness: Acts of kindness, compassion, charity and selfless service contribute to good karma. For example, helping others in need, being respectful to elders, and practicing non-violence are all considered actions that generate positive karma.

Spiritual Progress: In many karma traditions, good karma is seen as a means to advance spiritually. Accumulating good karma is thought to help one attain higher states of consciousness or, ultimately, break free from the cycle of reincarnation (samsara).

Examples: Donating to a charity, volunteering to help those less fortunate, being truthful and honest, and practicing acts of kindness are examples of actions that can generate good karma.

Bad Karma: Bad karma, also known as "Papa" or "Adharma," represents actions that are unwholesome, immoral, or harmful. These actions lead to unfavorable consequences and suffering. Here are some important aspects of bad karma:

Negative Outcomes: Bad karma often results in negative consequences, such as suffering, misfortune, illness, or unhappiness. It can also lead to challenging life circumstances.

Unethical Actions: Actions that harm others, deceive, manipulate, or engage in violence, contribute to bad karma. Breaking moral and ethical codes generally generates negative karma.

Karmic Debt: Bad karma is often seen as accumulating a karmic debt that one must eventually resolve or face in future lives. This may involve experiencing the consequences of one's actions in subsequent incarnations.

Examples: Engaging in dishonesty, harming others physically or emotionally, engaging in theft, or harboring ill intentions, are examples of actions that can generate bad karma.

It's important to note that karma is not a simplistic, one-to-one system and can be influenced by numerous factors, including intention, context, and the accumulation of both good and bad karma over multiple lifetimes. Additionally, the concept of karma is not limited to just the Hindu or Buddhist traditions; variations of it can be found in other cultures and belief systems as well.

Ultimately, understanding and working with the concept of karma involves striving to cultivate good karma through virtuous actions, while seeking to avoid bad karma through ethical conduct and self-awareness.

* * *

"Nishkama Karma" is a fundamental concept in Hindu philosophy, particularly in the context of Karma Yoga. It refers to the performance of actions without any attachment to the fruits or outcomes of those actions. The term "Nishkama" can be broken down into "Nish" (meaning "without") and "Kama" (meaning "desire"). Therefore, Nishkama Karma can be understood as "selfless action without desire."

Key aspects of Nishkama Karma include:

Selflessness: Nishkama Karma involves performing actions purely for the sake of duty, service, or the greater good, rather than for personal gain, recognition or selfish desires. This selflessness is a way of transcending the ego and acting with pure intentions.

Detachment: Practitioners of Nishkama Karma detach themselves from the outcomes or results of their actions. They understand that the world is governed by a complex web of cause and effect, and they have limited control over the results. Therefore, they focus solely on the quality and sincerity of their actions.

Surrender to the divine: Nishkama Karma often involves surrendering the results of one's actions to a higher power or the divine. It acknowledges that the ultimate outcome is beyond individual control and depends on the will of the divine or the cosmic order.

Equanimity: Practicing Nishkama Karma requires maintaining inner equanimity in the face of success or failure. One does not become elated when things go well or disheartened when they don't. This even-mindedness is an important aspect of this philosophy.

Self-Realization: Nishkama Karma is not just about selfless service; it is also a path to self-realization and spiritual growth. By performing actions without attachment to results, individuals can gradually transcend their ego and realize their inner divinity.

Here are a few examples to illustrate Nishkama Karma:

- A teacher who imparts knowledge to students without expecting praise, higher salaries, or awards is practicing Nishkama Karma. The teacher focuses on teaching to the best of their ability and lets go of attachment to external recognition.

- A doctor who treats patients with the utmost care and compassion, regardless of their ability to pay, practices Nishkama Karma. They prioritize the well-being of the patient above financial gain.

- A philanthropist who donates to charities without seeking public recognition or personal gain exemplifies Nishkama Karma. The act of giving is done out of a genuine desire to help those in need, without attachment to personal rewards.

- A farmer who works tirelessly to cultivate crops, acknowledging that the harvest may be affected by various factors beyond their control, practices Nishkama Karma. They understand that their duty is to work the land with dedication and let nature take its course.

Nishkama Karma is a profound spiritual concept that aligns with the idea of selfless service and the practice of Karma Yoga. It encourages individuals to act in the world with a sense of duty, love, and devotion, ultimately leading to spiritual growth and liberation from the cycle of karma.

"Karma Phala" (the fruits of karma). This concept can be better understood through the example of a temple ritual and the distribution of Prasad, which is the offering made to God during the worship ceremony. Let's elaborate on this idea:

The Action and the Doer:

In a temple, the priest plays the role of the doer. They meticulously prepare for and perform the pooja (worship ritual). The priest's actions include various tasks, such as cleaning the temple, offering prayers, lighting incense, and performing religious rites. The actions are performed with devotion and a sense of duty, embodying the doer's part of the equation. *Example*: The priest cleans the temple premises, arranges the altar, and chants sacred verses during the pooja.

The Results of the Action (Karma Phala):

The results of the action in this context are represented by Prasad, which is the food offering made to God. Prasad is believed to be imbued with divine blessings and is considered sacred. Devotees receive Prasad as a form of grace or divine blessings. They accept it with reverence and gratitude. *Example*: After the pooja, the priest offers fruits and other food items to the deity. Devotees receive a portion of this blessed offering as Prasad.

Accepting Outcomes with Grace:

The key idea here is to accept the results of actions (Karma Phala) with the same attitude as devotees accepting Prasad. Just as devotees cannot pick what Prasad they receive in life, if the fruit salad is offered to the God and distributed as Prasad, you cannot say, "I like mangoes and I don't want prunes," you accept whatever comes your way. Individuals should accept the outcomes that come their way with grace, humility and an understanding that these outcomes are divine blessings. *Example*: Imagine facing a setback at work or encountering a difficult personal situation. Instead of resisting or complaining, one accepts it as a part of their life's journey and learns to respond with patience and equanimity, like accepting Prasad with gratitude.

Converting Activities to Worship:

The broader message is to spiritualize your daily life by treating all your actions as acts of worship. By doing so, every task, no matter how mundane, is imbued with a sense of sacredness and devotion. This shift in perspective can bring about a profound change in your attitude and approach to life. *Example*: When you go to work, if you approach your tasks with dedication, integrity and the intention to serve others, you are essentially converting your professional responsibilities into a form of worship, and the results of your work become like divine blessings.

By adopting this perspective, individuals can cultivate a sense of contentment, equanimity, and spiritual growth in their everyday lives. They learn to accept the ups and downs of life as part of their spiritual journey, just as devotees accept Prasad without discrimination. This approach encourages an attitude of surrender to the divine will and a deeper understanding of the interconnectedness of all actions and their consequences.

* * *

Reincarnation: In many interpretations of the Law of Karma, the consequences of your actions can extend into future lives. Your actions in this life are believed to influence your circumstances in subsequent incarnations.

Now, let's relate these principles to your metaphor:

1. Doing Good Work and Being a Good Human:

In the metaphor, if you do good work and maintain moral integrity, you are rewarded in heaven. This mirrors the concept that good deeds (good karma) lead to positive consequences. The metaphorical "grand gold chain" symbolizes the positive results, which can include a fortunate existence or favorable circumstances.

2. Doing Ill Work and Harming Others:

Conversely, if you engage in harmful actions and negatively impact others, you face negative consequences. These actions can lead to being "handcuffed with a metal ring" and being sent to "prison," metaphorically representing the idea that bad karma results in suffering, challenges, or unfavorable life conditions.

3. Celebrating and Facilitating:

In the metaphor, the positive consequences are celebrated and facilitated in heaven, much like how society honors individuals who have made significant positive contributions by awarding them prizes and medals. This reflects the idea that good karma is recognized and rewarded, either in this life or in future lives.

4. Karma and Moral Responsibility:

The underlying message of this metaphor aligns with the concept of moral responsibility inherent in the Law of Karma. It emphasizes that individuals have the power to shape their destinies through their actions, and the consequences of these actions are a reflection of their character and choices.

It's important to note that, while the metaphor provides a vivid and accessible way to understand the concept of karma, the traditional interpretation of karma is more complex and multifaceted. It involves an intricate interplay of actions, intentions, and the nature of the individual's consciousness.

In summary, the Law of Karma is a belief in the consequences of one's actions, with good deeds leading to positive results and bad deeds leading to negative outcomes. Your metaphor creatively captures this idea, using the symbolism of heaven, prison and rewards to illustrate how moral actions are celebrated, and immoral actions are penalized.

* * *

Karma is a complex concept rooted in various Eastern philosophies and religions, such as Hinduism, Buddhism, and Jainism. It revolves around the idea that every action, intention or thought has consequences, and individuals accrue a kind of "moral scorecard" based on their deeds. Two related concepts within the framework of karma are "karma debt" and "karma accumulation."

1. Karma Debt:

Definition: Karma debt refers to the negative consequences or "debts" that a person incurs as a result of harmful actions, intentions, or thoughts. It suggests that negative karma is akin to a burden or an obligation that needs to be balanced.

Cause: When individuals engage in actions that harm others, act dishonestly, or cause suffering, they accumulate negative karma, creating a debt that must be "paid off" in the future. This can lead to unfavorable circumstances or difficulties in life.

Resolution: Resolving or paying off karma debt typically involves engaging in positive actions and intentions to counteract the negative effects. This process is often associated with moral growth, redemption, and spiritual development.

2. Karma Accumulation:

Definition: Karma accumulation refers to the overall sum or balance of one's karma, which encompasses both positive and negative consequences of actions, intentions, and thoughts.

Cause: Karma accumulation is the result of all actions, whether good or bad, that an individual engages in throughout their life. Positive actions lead to positive karma, while negative actions lead to negative karma.

Impact: The accumulated karma can influence an individual's current and future experiences, circumstances and relationships. It plays a significant role in shaping one's life path and spiritual evolution.

It's important to note that the concept of karma is not deterministic, but rather serves as a guideline for understanding the consequences of one's choices and actions. Additionally, beliefs about karma and how it operates may vary among different cultures and philosophical traditions. Some believe that the effects of karma can extend beyond a single lifetime, affecting future rebirths, while others interpret it in a more secular or psychological context, emphasizing the consequences of one's actions in this lifetime.

In summary, karma debt and karma accumulation are concepts within the framework of karma that refer to the negative consequences of harmful actions and the overall balance of an individual's actions, intentions and thoughts, respectively. These concepts reflect the idea that our deeds have repercussions and can influence our present and future experiences.

* * *

Once upon a time, I went on a pilgrimage that changed my view of life forever. As I traveled from one sacred place to another, I felt awe and reverence. I didn't know that an unexpected encounter would challenge my beliefs and touch my soul deeply.

Among the crowd of pilgrims, I noticed a man who seemed out of place. His sharp eyes scanned the crowd and their belongings. Curiosity made me look at him, and to my surprise, I smiled warmly at him.

Curious, the man approached me cautiously. Seeing his unease, I greeted him warmly and asked how he was doing. With a hint of sadness, he replied, "Not very good. Times have changed. With all these new technologies and CCTV cameras everywhere, there's hardly anything left for me to steal."

I couldn't help but chuckle at his honest confession. Amused, he smiled back, and in that moment, we connected. "We are in a similar situation," I said. "I have nothing of value for you to take, and you have nothing to give me." We laughed together, feeling like kindred spirits.

Feeling a bond, the thief leaned toward me and whispered, "I'm heading to the bus stand. There are no CCTV cameras there." His eyes gleamed mischievously. But before he could leave, I felt the need to share something important.

I told him, "Listen, my friend. You might be surprised to know there are two hidden cameras, even at the bus stand."

Confused, he asked, "Did they just install them? I didn't see them last time."

Smiling, I replied, "No, my dear thief. These cameras are invisible. One is near your heart, above your soul, and the other watches from above. They can see your thoughts."

For a moment, we were silent as he took in my words. Overwhelmed, the thief fell to his knees, humbled and remorseful. He said, "Take me to your ashram. I want to help you and atone for my past. Give me any task, and I will dedicate my life to becoming a better person."

Moved by his sincerity, I helped him up. "You don't need to prove anything to me," I said gently. "Your transformation has already begun. Your encounter with the invisible cameras has changed your life forever."

The thief embraced his new purpose and started a journey of redemption. Today, he is a monk in our monastery, a living example of the power of perspective. Before anyone leaves on a pilgrimage, he checks their belongings, reminding them of the importance of security.

In his heart, he carries the memory of that encounter, forever changed by a single sentence. The thief turned monk shows that life's challenges can lead to profound transformations. No longer bound by his past, he now protects others, carrying the lesson of the invisible cameras with him always.

* * *

Arjun says, "Master, I have no interest in this conversation. I don't want to die; I want to transform and be a good human. Then, when the time comes, I will surrender to death. Master, please do something."

Master continues and says, "Don't worry. The pilot will make an announcement shortly that the engine is responding, and we will land safely." Master took a deep breath, and the pilot made the announcement.

The pilot says, "Ladies and gentlemen, your prayers have been heard. The engine is responding well, and we shall land safely."

Arjun said, "Master, thank you so much for saving all the souls on this aircraft. How did you visualize things ahead of us?"

Master said, "Arjun, the mind is a serene lake. A calm and tranquil mind is comparable to a peaceful lake. Just as a serene lake reflects the beauty around it and allows for clear visibility, a peaceful mind is thought to have clarity, focus and the ability to perceive thoughts and emotions without being disturbed by them."

The serene mind is free from agitation, stress, and mental turbulence. It is a state characterized by inner peace, equanimity, and harmony. This concept is often emphasized in meditation and mindfulness practices, where the aim is to cultivate a calm and still mind that can perceive reality as it is, undisturbed by the ever-changing thoughts and distractions. If the lake is clear, you can see the bottom of the lake. If the lake is muddied, you cannot see the bottom.

Did you notice the calmness of the pilot? He didn't panic; he was technically reviewing the system, and he was successful. He is a great leader; he saved the lives of people, not me. You should be a great leader in your family, work, life and health.

The lamp holds a special place in our culture. Spiritual leaders often refer to it as a symbol of an everlasting, bright flame that spreads light everywhere, without any smoke. This light symbolizes our inner consciousness, which brightens our thoughts and perception. It helps us see the world around us clearly, recognizing its beauty and endless possibilities.

Yet, the clarity of our perception depends on the state of our mind. Just like a lamp's flame can be smoky or steady, our thoughts can be positive or filled with negativity. The ancient sages advise us to purify our minds, making them steady and clear like the flame of a lamp in a calm place, banishing darkness around it.

Our minds are constantly filled with various thoughts, some uplifting, and others dragging us down. A positive mind sees beauty and wonder in everything, spreading joy and happiness to those around us.

It's often said that a focused and pure mind can achieve anything. Our mind shapes our reality. When it's filled with knowledge and clarity, we can act effectively and achieve our goals. But when it's clouded and uncertain, our perception of the world becomes distorted, leading to doubt and inefficiency in our actions.

Life is a mix of smooth highway journeys and unexpected rocky terrain with obstacles. These challenges often reflect our inner thoughts and beliefs. That's why it's important to be self-aware and introspective. By looking within, we can discover our true selves amidst the clutter of our thoughts. Though this process may initially reveal negativity and imperfections, it's crucial for growth and self-discovery.

When we let go of these negative thoughts, we uncover the brilliant light of our true selves. This light illuminates the world around us, filling it with opportunities, goodness, and wonder. With this newfound clarity, we gain the courage to face life's challenges with faith and bravery.

Let me tell you my favorite story of my favorite man.

* * *

15

The Great Leader, Dr. Abdul Kalam

It was a clear morning on Sriharikota Island, the launch site, on 10th August 1979. Top scientists, including the Indian Scientific Research Organization (ISRO) chairperson Prof. Satish Dhawan, were present at the venue. The project director was Dr APJ Abdul Kalam. Thousands of people had worked day and night for this project.

They set the rocket to launch and were ready at the launch pad. Announcements started, T minus 5 mins, T minus 4 mins, T minus 40 seconds. System alarm was raised: do not launch the rocket; there is a leakage in the control system. Dr. Kalam and the team calculated and assessed they have enough fuel, considering the leakage, to reach the orbit. Dr. Kalam took a decision consulting the team; they bypassed the system and launched the rocket.

SLV-3 had a beautiful lift-off at 7.48 a.m. as it left behind a thick trail of vapor. For 68 seconds, the vehicle soared along the predicted course to a height of 23 kms. Then came the fatal malfunction in the second stage control system. The rocket, instead of reaching the orbit, landed at the Bay of Bengal.

The world media witnessed the whole scene, including the political big wings. Dr. Kalam was dejected by the turn of events. Then walks Dr Satish Dhawan and tells Dr Kalam, "We have to attend the press conference." Dr Kalam got scared looking at the huge press presence of press reporters. Dr Satish Dhawan addressed the media and said, "Dear friends, we have failed today. I want to support my technologists, scientists and staff. They worked really hard. Please give them some time; they will definitely succeed. I take complete ownership of this failure."

After 11 months, on July 18, 1980, the team put in extraordinary efforts and is ready for the relaunch of SLV-3. This time they are successful, and the rocket is launched into orbit. Dr. Satish Dhawan walks toward Dr. Abdul Kalam and congratulates him. Dr. Kalam eagerly invites Dr. Satish Dhawan for a press conference. Dr. Satish Dhawan says, "It's your success. You go and handle it." When failure occurred, the leader took it upon his own shoulders. When success came, he gives it to his team.

If you look at M.S. Dhoni, he will always take tough decisions on the ground and tough questions at a press conference, and give the winning trophy to the youngsters on his team. If you can understand the moral of this story, you can be a great leader.

* * *

"You have great skills, master, yet you are not proud of anything. If I had these skills, I would have ruled the world." Arjun said.

* * *

During a casual conversation, Arjun asks Lord Krishna, "Why did monkeys labor so hard to build the bridge to Lanka? I would have done this with one arrow." Looking at Arjun's pride, Lord Krishna told Arjun, "Build the bridge." Arjun, with the help of Gandiv (his bow), constructs the bridge. Lord Krishna calls Hanuman to test the bridge. The moment Hanuman takes the first step, the bridge crumbles and falls apart. Lord Krishna says, "Never be proud of your skills."

One of the hallmarks of a humble person is their ability to be grounded. In fact, we often refer to proud people as air-headed, as described in the above story of Arjuna. If you give careful thought about what makes people connected to the ground and air, it's all about energy management.

We are all aware of electrical grounding. When the electrician does the wiring of your house, office or factory, he installs one wire called earthing. Earthing is the transferring and immediate discharge of electrical energy to the Earth through a low-resistance wire. Likewise, electricity is everywhere, even in the human body. Our cells are specialized in conducting electrical currents. Electricity is required for the nervous system to send signals throughout the body and to the brain.

Your body can handle a certain amount of energy. If the electrical charge in your body increases, you either need to improve your ability to handle that charge or go about releasing that excess charge into the Earth. The lower part of the body is the entry for a lot of the magnetic energy or "Earth grounding" energy, and the top of the head and back of the neck is the usual doorway for the electrical or "sky grounding" energy. In you, Earth and sky meet and mingle. It is your nature to blend these two as fuel for your life on this planet.

The technique of grounding: when you feel you have an excess amount of energy, you need to sit on the ground and release it. You need to acknowledge that you have evolved from the ground and you are not this body, not the mind, but a pure soul.

* * *

Arjun said, "Master, I promise I will remain grounded. You have saved me from crashing. Can you please tell me the traits of a great person and a person who had a great downfall? I will pin this to my heart and remain great, and make progress to become a great human, and remain careful of my mind and senses, pulling toward the worldly things and causing a downfall in my life. I would like to pin this answer to my heart and swear by it."

Master said, "Great question, Arjun. By asking this question, your winnability in life has increased many fold. If you understand the answer and live by it, you will have the best life ahead. Listen carefully as I invoke a verse from the Bhagavad Gita."

* * *

Dhyāyato vishayān pumsah, sangas teshūpajāyate.
sangāt sañjāyate, kāmah, kāmāt, krodho bhijāyate
Krodhād bhavati sammohã, sammohāt smṛiti-vibhramãh.
smṛiti-bhranśhād, buddhi-nāśho, buddhi-nāśhāt praṇaśhyati

As a man contemplates sense objects, attachment for them arises. From attachment, a desire for them will be born. From desire arises anger. From anger comes delusion. From delusion comes the loss of memory. From loss of memory comes destruction of discrimination, and from destruction of discrimination, he perishes.

At first, the man may not have any attachment to anything, but gradually the senses, prompted by past samskaras, settle on a particular object and the mind begins to contemplate it. So, a kind of contact is established between the mind and that object, the senses being the connecting link. The object may be anything from the fashionable piece of dress to the glamor and glory of an emperor. That contact becomes stronger and stronger, and a deeply felt desire arises to possess and enjoy that object.

This is *Kama*. It is the worst enemy of man. *Mahapapam* (all sinful)—such is the Lord's'description of Kama. When Kama enters the mind, it is like a reptile moving about in the house. The occupants of that house live in horrible dread, and there is every danger of their being stung and killed. Such indeed is the destructive power of Kama when it enters the human heart.

It is indeed better to stop it before it enters the mind. But if it enters stealthily, the moment one discovers it, he should throw it out with all the power at his command.

Otherwise, the Kama, in its wake, will bring his associates, friends and other destructive forces like Krodha and throw down the unfortunate man into destruction. All this is vividly described by the teacher of the Gita. Let the seeker know who his enemies are, how they work, how they tempt, how they subdue, and how they finally destroy man.

When Kama enters the mind, just behind him comes Krodha. These two are eternal associates of evil. One cannot be without the other. Such is the closeness of their intimacy. The frustration of desire causes anger and hatred. Krodha is like powerful alcohol. Passion, like poison, fills the whole personality. He trembles and shivers all over the body, the eyes become bloodshot, speech becomes incoherent, abuse and violence are indulged in, and the human being is transformed into a wild animal that is deprived of a piece of flesh when it is hungry. He behaves like a man possessed by an evil spirit. So it is said here that delusion (sammoha) overpowers him by anger (Krodha). Delusion causes loss of memory.

The deluded man, fired with anger, forgets the people with whom he is dealing. Be he a father, Guru or friend; the angry man abuses him and strikes him down. For the time being, he forgets the status of the person, honor for the father, reverence for the Guru, affection for the friend. This is loss of memory (smritivibramah) of one's self. So long as a man holds on to the Self, anger cannot overpower him. But the moment that memory of his true self is lost, man becomes a beast.

From the loss of memory, discrimination of right and wrong is lost. By the destruction of the grinding intellect, man perishes. Therefore, the Lord warns the aspirant to keep himself away from sensing objects and to practice self-control.

Contemplating the objects of the senses: It is important to note that the word contemplation is used in this context. Contemplation is not a new faculty to be acquired. Every man is constantly in a state of contemplation. Some contemplate wealth, others the pleasure of wine, others the pleasures of sex, others the dignity of position, name and fame. So the world moves on, each one attached to a particular desire, meditating on it, and trying to realize it as much as possible. So contemplation is the natural faculty of the mind. The wise man, who has understood the worthlessness of worldly pleasures, turns his mind to God and contemplates the purity and glory of God. He attains pure joy and endless peace.

What is required is that the same power of contemplation that runs after worldly objects should be given a new direction toward a spiritual aim. We come across stories of men immersed in sensuality suddenly turning out to be pure devotees of God. What happens in such cases is that the man, by some cause or other, discovers the filthy nature of sensual pleasures and turns away from them, and the mind naturally runs for the pure and perfect, with the same force and momentum as it formerly had for sense pleasures. The point is contemplation should be directed toward Atma and not toward sense objects. Prahlada asked the Lord for the same boon, that his mind may always be fixed in the Lord and not in the ephemeral world.

16

Saintly Virtues

Master said, "Now, let's learn about saintly virtues."

abhayaṁ sattva-sanśhuddhir, jñāna-yoga-vyavasthitiḥ
dānaṁ, damaśh, cha yajñaśh, cha, svādhyāyas, tapa, ārjavam
ahinsā, satyam, akrodhas, tyāgaḥ, śhāntir, apaiṣhunam
dayā bhūteṣhv, aloluptvaṁ, mārdavaṁ, hrīr, achāpalam
Tejaḥ kṣhamā dhṛitiḥ, śhaucham adroho nāti-mānitā
Bhavanti sampadaṁ, daivīm abhijātasya, bhārata.

The Supreme divine Personality said: O scion of Bharat, these are the saintly virtues of those endowed with a divine nature—fearlessness, purity of mind, steadfastness in spiritual knowledge, charity, control of the senses, sacrifice, study of the sacred books, austerity and straightforwardness; non-violence, truthfulness, absence of anger, renunciation, peacefulness, restraint from fault-finding, compassion toward all living beings, absence of covetousness, gentleness, modesty and lack of fickleness, vigor, forgiveness, fortitude, cleanliness, bearing enmity toward none, and absence of vanity.

* * *

Commentary

Here, Shree Krishna describes twenty-six virtues of a saintly nature. These should be cultivated as a part of our spiritual practice for elevating ourselves to the supreme goal.

1. **Fearlessness**. It is the state of freedom from concern for present and future miseries. Inordinate attachment of any kind causes fear. Attachment to wealth leads to dreading impoverishment; attachment to social prestige causes fearing infamy; attachment to vice leads to anxiety about sin's consequences; attachment to bodily comfort causes fearing ill-health, and so on. Detachment and surrender to God vanquish all fear from the heart.

2. **Purity of mind**. This is the state of inner cleanliness. The mind generates and harbors thoughts, sentiments, feelings, emotions, etc. When these are

ethical, wholesome, positive, and uplifting, the mind is considered pure, and when they are unethical and degrading, the mind is considered impure. Attachment to objects in the modes of passion and ignorance contaminates the mind, while attachment to God purifies it.

3. **Steadfastness in spiritual knowledge**. It is said: tattva vismaraṇāt bhekivat. *"When human beings forget what is right and what is wrong, they become like animals."* Thus, the path of virtue is forged by remaining steadfast in the awareness of spiritual principles.

4. **Charity**. It refers to the giving away of one's possessions for a good cause or to needy persons. True charity is that which is done not with a feeling of superiority but with a sense of gratefulness to God for the opportunity to help. Material charity, done for the welfare of the body, helps others temporarily. Spiritual charity done on the platform of the soul helps eliminate the cause of all suffering, which is separation from God. Consequently, it is considered higher than material charity.

5. **Control of the senses.** The senses are notorious in their ability to drag the mind deeper into material illusion. They tempt the living being to seek

immediate gratification. However, walking the path of virtue requires forsaking the lower sensual pleasures to achieve the higher goal. Thus, restraint of the senses is an essential virtue for treading the path to God.

6. **Sacrifice**. It means executing one's Vedic duties and social obligations, even though they may not be enjoyable. Sacrifice is considered perfect when it is done for the pleasure of God.

7. **Study of the sacred books**. It is an important aspect of cultivating the divine nature. To feed the intellect with uplifting knowledge from the scriptures is crucial. When the intellect is illumined with proper knowledge, one's actions naturally become sublime.

8. **Austerity**. The body-mind-senses are such that, if we pamper them, they become pleasure-seeking, but if we restrain them, they become disciplined. Thus, austerity is the voluntary acceptance of hardships for purifying the body, mind, and intellect.

9. **Straightforwardness**. Simplicity in speech and conduct unclutters the mind and engenders the sprouting of noble thoughts. The English phrase "simple living, high thinking," aptly expresses the benefits of the virtue of straightforwardness.

10. **Non-violence**. It means not impeding the progressive life of other living beings through thought, word or deed.

11. **Truthfulness.** It means restraining oneself from distorting facts to suit one's purpose. God is the Absolute Truth, and hence the practice of truthfulness takes us toward him; on the other hand, falsehood, while convenient, takes us away from God.

12. **Absence of anger**. The manifestation of anger is a defect of the material mind. It occurs when the desires for happiness are obstructed, and things do not turn out as one envisaged. By developing detachment and surrender to the will of God, one overcomes anger.

13. **Renunciation**. The entire material energy belongs to God, and it is meant for His pleasure. Hence, the opulences of the world are not for one's enjoyment, but for being utilized in the service of God. To be fixed in this understanding is renunciation.

14. **Peacefulness**. The cultivation of virtue requires mental poise. Peacefulness is the ability to retain inner equilibrium despite disturbing external situations.

15. **Restraint from fault-finding.** The whole world and everything in it is a mixture of good and bad

qualities. Focusing on defects in others dirties our mind, while focusing on their virtues purifies it. The nature of a saintly person is to see his or her own defects and observe the virtues of others.

16. **Compassion toward all living beings**. As individuals evolve spiritually, they naturally rise above self-centeredness and develop empathy for all living beings. Compassion is the deep sympathy that arises upon seeing the sufferings of others.

17. **Absence of covetousness**. Greed is the desire to accumulate more than what one legitimately needs for the maintenance of the body. Under its sway, people acquire huge amounts of wealth and possessions, though they know that at the time of death, everything will be left behind. Freedom from such covetousness leads to contentment and inner peace.

18. **Gentleness**. The disposition of behaving roughly with others arises from insensitivity to their feelings. But as one grows in spiritual stature, one naturally sheds crudeness in behavior. Gentleness is a sign of spiritual refinement.

19. **Modesty**. Hrīḥ means "sense of guilt in performing actions contrary to the injunctions of scriptures

and society." The saintly nature is imbued with a ruthless inner conscience that gives one a sense of guilt for committing sinful acts.

20. **Lack of fickleness**. We may begin with good intentions, but if we get distracted by temptations and hardships, we cannot complete the journey. Success on the path of virtue comes by unwaveringly pursuing the goal despite all diversions that come along the way.

21. **Vigor**. From purity of mind comes a deep inner drive to act according to one's values and beliefs. Hence, saintly personalities bring immense power and vigor to the tasks they pursue.

22. **Forgiveness or forbearance**. This is the ability to tolerate the offenses of others without feeling the need to retaliate. Through forgiveness, one heals the emotional wounds caused by others that would otherwise fester and disturb the mind.

23. **Fortitude**. It is the inner strength and determination in pursuing the goal, even when the mind and senses are wearied due to unfavorable circumstances. Most of the important things in the world have been accomplished by people who kept on trying when there seemed to be no hope at all. Sri Aurobindo put this very eloquently: "You have to be more persistent than the difficulty; there is no other way. "

24. **Cleanliness**. It refers to both internal and external purity. Virtuous people believe in maintaining external cleanliness because it is conducive to internal purity. George Bernard Shaw said, "Better keep yourself clean and bright; you are the window through which you must see the world. "

25. **Bearing enmity toward none.** Bearing enmity toward others poisons our own mind, and this becomes an impediment in the path of spiritual progress. The quality of freedom from hatred toward others is developed by realizing that they are also like us, and that God resides in all.

26. **Absence of vanity**. Self-praise, boastfulness, ostentation, etc., all stem from pride. Saintly personalities see nothing in themselves to be proud of, but instead feel gratitude to God for the good qualities they possess. Thus, they refrain from self-aggrandizement.

* * *

17

Lift as You Rise

Master said, "Arjun, it looks like the captain has kept his promise, and what a perfect landing. I should see him and thank him. After saying whatever I have said, think about it, and analyze it. Only if you think it's right, follow it. If it helps you, help others. Make a list of people who may need your help and choose at least one person to help. By investing our energy in empathy, love and kindness the first thing in the morning, we will feel that same energy for ourselves throughout the day. Everyone is going through a battle we know nothing about. Make a resolution that you will try to be kind to yourself and every person you meet. Not only will this boost your endorphins in the morning, but it will also attract people into your life who will wish the best for you. "

Arjun says, "Master, thank you for the profound teaching. I shall act according to your instructions." The central theme of your teaching is that my emotions cannot come in the way of me performing my duties. Inaction is better than action. Perform my duties without getting attached to the results.

Master says, "Arjun, you are an artificial intelligence, machine learning and robotics professional. Whatever I have said, you can generate all the above and much more with a click of a button. But you remained humble listening to my talk. Everyone can teach this or generate via AI. It will all boil down to one thing. Hear me out loud and clear. It's implementation. Implementing the learning every single day and make the teacher proud of his student."

"Arjun, you are very dear to me. Blessing you for living till 100 with full of energy and without illness. May you be a marvelous man on this planet. Or simply being so healthy that you get very good things done, enjoy every moment with those you love, and contribute to the making of a much better world."

"After my talk, if you had given me a standing ovation and said, 'Look, ladies and gentlemen, he is the best speaker I have ever come across,' I would have been ashamed of that. You understood the teaching and said, 'I shall act according to your instructions; I am delighted.' I am reminded of a song by the great Tamil poet, Kannadasan. Follow the lyrics carefully; it's a profound teaching. First, I have the Tamil words followed by English translation."

Manidan embavan deivam agala
A human can become a God.
Vari vari vazhangupodhu, vallal agalam.
Valai pola thannai thanthu, thyagi agalam.
Urugi odum melagu pola olaiyaai veesalam.
Manam manam adhu kovil agalam

* * *

A human can become a God. When humans give wholeheartedly and expect nothing in return, they truly become noble figures in their own right. Similarly, just like a banana tree, which possesses usefulness in every part, this kind of selfless giving symbolizes the highest form of sacrifice. By sacrificing for the betterment of others, one can leave a lasting impact and be remembered as a truly remarkable individual. They have the power to radiate positivity and goodness, much like the wax in a candle that selflessly melts away to illuminate its surroundings. The mind has the potential to transform into a temple.

Kannadasan, born as Muthiah, was a famous Tamil poet, lyricist and scriptwriter in the South Indian film industry. He was born on June 24, 1927, and passed away on October 17, 1981. Kannadasan is known for his powerful and evocative writing, exploring a wide range of themes, such as love, philosophy, spirituality, and social issues.

His work spans across various artistic mediums, including poetry, song lyrics and film scripts. Kannadasan's poetic style was known for its simplicity and accessibility, making his verses relatable to a wide audience. His lyrics in Tamil films were often regarded as poetic gems, and he collaborated with renowned music composers such as M. S. Viswanathan and K. V. Mahadevan to create memorable songs.

Despite being a remarkable scholar, his inability to overcome his addiction to alcohol led to his untimely demise at the age of fifty- four. It is deeply concerning that such a brilliant individual was taken from us too soon, yet his profound songs and teachings will undoubtedly endure for eternity.

* * *

Master says, "I am deeply concerned because young individuals in various fields aspire to imitate their masters in every aspect of their lives. They may even believe that by consuming alcohol or other substances like their masters, they can become great scholars, artists, too. It is disturbing to think that they may think it is acceptable to indulge in such behavior in order to achieve greatness."

"However, my concern goes beyond the specific issue of alcohol or drugs, as I am referring to addiction. As a master, one must exercise extreme caution in their actions, as this also applies to parents. Arjun, teach the best to your kids and be a great parent. I am sure you will be a great parent. I can visualize telling this story to your kids."

Arjun said, "Master, I am amazed by the lyrics of this song. It says humans can become like God. I have a question, and I hope you won't be mad at me for asking this after your spiritual discourse. Does God really exist?"

The Master replied, "Good question, Arjun. At the beginning of my spiritual journey, my friend and I attended a spiritual retreat. When we returned, there was heavy rain and flooding due to a cyclone, and the roof of our ashram disappeared. I said, 'Thank you, God. You have made our lives easier by removing the roof, considering our open environment at the venue of our spiritual retreat. Lord, you are my Lord, and you always do the best for me.'"

My friend was deeply annoyed.

He said, 'We went on a spiritual quest, prayed, and were devoted souls. Why did this happen to us? If God exists, our lives should be better.'

I just lay down in a corner and went to sleep. It started to drizzle, and my friend angrily walked outside. I followed him and asked what was wrong.

He said, 'It's raining. How can we sleep now?'

I replied, 'Lord, you are my Lord, and you always will be. Considering we haven't bathed for a few days, you are blessing us with raindrops. I am truly grateful to you. Lord, you are always my Lord, and you will do everything for my good.'

My friend got even more annoyed and said, 'What is this "Lord, you are always my Lord"? So many bad things are happening, and you keep saying the same thing. We attended the discourse, and our lives were supposed to be better.'

I said, 'My life is better because I received the teaching from the guru straight to my heart, which says, *"A complaining mind is never peaceful; a grateful heart is always peaceful."* I don't know if God exists, but this non-complaining and ever-grateful attitude keeps me peaceful. I will not trade this peace for a roof over the ashram. This is the greatest lesson I have learned during the spiritual retreat.'

By then, the rain had stopped, and a cool breeze set in. My friend nodded in agreement and said, 'You are right.

We should be non-complaining and at peace always.' He went to sleep and slept peacefully, like a baby. The spiritual discourse was given by *Mahatria Ra,* one of my gurus and a great spiritual teacher. He explains things beautifully. Master said to Arjun, "I don't even know if God exists. True masters will tell you this. However, worshipping and being grateful for life is the best thing to do. And this attitude toward life will keep you peaceful, blissful, and content.

Master said, "Arjun, visualize the best thing, and the best will happen to you. Visualization serves as your mind's personal cinema, your own private movie theater. You have the choice to project continually, either a negative or a positive film, as desired. Even if I were to replay your preferred movie twice, you might not find it enjoyable. On the third viewing, it could become tedious, and who knows what would happen on the fourth. Nevertheless, you tend to visualize past events from years ago vividly and in great detail, frequently dwelling on them, despite their being beyond your control.

Let me tell you a story

* * *

Once, in New York, my friend took me to an Indian restaurant that served South Indian meals on banana leaves. He spoke very highly of the place, saying his last meal there was wonderful and a must-try. The restaurant was far, and the traffic was heavy, but we made a reservation and went. Despite the reservation, the restaurant was full, and we had to wait. When we finally got our food, it was average and not as great as my friend had described.

My friend was furious with the restaurant management for not handling the reservation well and not serving their best. On the way back, my friend kept apologizing for the not-so-great experience. I told him it was alright, but he insisted that last time it had been awesome and complained about the restaurant for an hour. He had praised the restaurant on the way there, but complained for over an hour on the way back.

I told him, "Don't get too excited about anything in this world, and don't get too upset over one meal and ruin your day. If the food is great, say it's good. If it's not, say it's alright and move on. You'll feel better. Even though the food was okay for me, your one-hour explanation left a bitter taste in my mouth. Someone else might have had a great experience and posted about it online, which is why the crowd was there. The restaurant management probably didn't anticipate the crowd and failed in the customer experience. Excuse them and move on with your life. Don't get stuck on one bad experience."

* * *

18

Technique for Revisiting Unpleasant Past Memories:

Imagine a small screen on your mental canvas, perhaps the tiniest screen in existence. Begin by switching off the lights, and as you play the memory, envision it in black and white. Let the images become distorted, and the audio grow faint. Now, introduce an element of distraction, as if someone suddenly opens the door, making the whole experience unsettling.

If you're repeatedly revisiting a negative event from, say, 1952 and you're visualizing it in vivid colors, will it be of any benefit? It's akin to preparing an unpleasant dish; why subject yourself to it more than once or even multiple times? You know it's bound to have a bitter taste.

Visualization Technique for a Positive Future Event:

Imagine on your mental movie screen, which happens to be the most impressive screen imaginable. It's a vast screen, so please put on your 3D glasses to enhance the experience. Get ready for something truly incredible. Envision the most wonderful moments of your life with vibrant colors and immersive surround sound, and complement them with fantastic background music. And don't forget to add applause whenever it's appropriate.

There is an old simile in India that if you place a cup of milk before a Raja Hamsa (Swan) with plenty of water in it, it will take all the milk and leave the water. In that way, you should take what is of value in knowledge from the master and leave the dross.

* * *

Arjun says,

> *"Today, I recognize t*

> *e profound power of words to shape lives, challenge beliefs, and ignite transformation."*

> *"I am open and receptive to the wisdom before me, knowing it holds the key to a more fulfilling and purposeful life."*

"This teaching invites me to reflect, grow, and align my choices with truths that elevate my existence."

"I embrace the courage to shed fears and limitations, stepping into a life of authenticity and abundance."

"With gratitude in my heart, I allow these lessons to illuminate my path and guide my every action."

"This is the start of a new chapter, where growth, self-awareness, and inner peace become my foundation."

"By internalizing this wisdom, I unlock the potential for transformation, self-discovery, and endless possibilities."

"I welcome the teachings that inspire me to live a life aligned with purpose, joy and fulfillment."

"Today, I choose growth, courage and the clarity to create a reality that reflects my truest self."

"Through these lessons, I find the strength to overcome challenges and embrace a life of boundless potential."

As I sat in the airplane, ready for take-off, little did I know that my greatest entertainment and enlightenment would come from within. The journey I was about to embark on was not just a physical one, but a spiritual and intellectual one as well.

As the plane soared through the sky, I embarked on a journey of self-discovery and growth. The master, a wise and insightful being, shared with me stories of his own personal experiences and the lessons he had learned along the way. They spoke of triumphs and failures, laughter and tears,

Love and heartbreak.

His words carried a profound wisdom that resonated deep within me. I found myself captivated by his stories, each one presenting a new perspective and a new lesson to be learned. It was as if I was watching a movie, with each story unfolding before my eyes.

There were tales of courage and determination, where individuals overcame seemingly insurmountable obstacles to achieve their dreams. I was inspired by their resilience and their unwavering belief in themselves.

There were moments of laughter and joy where the master shared anecdotes that brought smiles to our faces. These stories reminded me of the importance of finding humor and lightness in even the most challenging situations.

But there were also tragedies, heart-wrenching tales of loss and suffering. These stories touched a deep part of my soul, evoking empathy and compassion. I realized the importance of embracing both the joys and.

sorrows of life, as they are the threads that make up the tapestry of our existence.

The master's words were like a symphony, each story adding a new layer to the melody. They challenged my beliefs, expanded my perspectives, and encouraged me to question the status quo.

At that moment, I realized that true enlightenment is not found in external sources of entertainment, but within ourselves. It is through introspection, reflection, and the pursuit of knowledge that we are able to.

Deepen our understanding of the world and our place in it.

As the plane descended, I felt a profound sense of gratitude for the unexpected in-flight enlightenment I had received. I knew that this experience had changed me, leaving an indelible mark on my journey to self-discovery and personal growth.

And so, as I stepped off the plane, I carried with me the stories and lessons shared by the master. They would continue to guide me on my path, reminding me to seek truth, embrace challenges, and live a life filled with purpose and meaning. The in-flight enlightenment I had found was far more valuable than any entertainment I could have hoped for.

I am grateful for this opportunity to enhance my life through this teaching. I am ready for the positive changes and endless possibilities that lie ahead. Today, I embrace the transformative power of this teaching and allow it to illuminate my path toward a more authentic and purposeful existence.

* * *

Arjun says, "Master, I have been calling you 'master' throughout. I didn't even ask your name. May I know your name?"

Master says, "My name is Sacchidanand. The word Sacchidanand is formed from the union of three words: sat or truth, chit, or consciousness, and anand or bliss. You are also Sacchidanand—existence, consciousness, and bliss. I have realized this, and you will also realize this shortly."

Arjun says, "Master, how do I reach you? I need to learn more from you."

The Master said, "When you are ready for the next level of teaching, the Master will appear in front of you, Arjun."

Arjun said, "No, Master, I want to meet you tomorrow and attain the next level of learning."

The Master said, "It reminds me of an ant which discovers a sugar mountain. After taking one grain of sugar, while going back to its hut, the ant said, 'I am coming back for the entire mountain.' First, the ant has to digest the grain of sugar. Likewise, implement what you have learned. I will appear at the right time."

Upon reaching the terminal, Arjun says, "Master, please wait for me. I need to use the restroom due to the effect of consuming beers. I want to take your blessings."

The master smiles at Arjun. Arjun comes out of the restroom, but the master was not there. Arjun thought the master must have gone to the belt to collect the luggage. Arjun runs to the luggage belt. He doesn't see the master and enquires with the fellow passengers about the monk. The passengers nod their heads. One passenger tells Arjun, "I think monks don't have bondage and baggage; you are looking in the wrong place."

Arjun runs toward the airport authorities and asks them about the passenger sitting at seat 7A. The airport authorities say, "So many flights come with so many passengers. How can we answer you? We are not supposed to give passenger information to fellow passengers."

Arjun protests and heads toward the airport manager's cabin and tells him how his life changed with spirituality after boarding the flight. He hoped to fall at the feet of the master and take his blessing. The airport manager pulls the flight details, seems surprised, and calls the flight in-charge. The flight in-charge reaches the airport manager's cabin, and the airport manager checks with the flight in-charge about the passenger seated at 7A.

The flight in-charge looks at Arjun and says, "Sir, I hope you are alright? The seat 7A was empty; the passenger named Sachidananda missed the aircraft. I thought you would have the pleasure of flying by the window, but you didn't move; the seat was vacant the whole time."

Airport manager asks the flight in-charge "How much drink did you serve him? Looks like the gentleman was high on liquid spirituality."

The flight in-charge says, "Negative, sir, he didn't consume any alcohol, and he changed his meal preference to vegetarian and skipped the desserts. He was quiet and well-behaved, occasionally staring at me."

* * *

Arjun Singh recounted to his sons. "I walked back from the airport, feeling dejected, and took a taxi home. In that moment, I made a solemn vow to the master in my mind: 'Whatever you have taught me, I swear to follow it until my last breath, and I will pass this wisdom on to future generations.'"

Bob nodded in agreement, while Abhimanyu's eyes filled with tears.

Abhimanyu then said to his father, "Dad, I have never met the master, and I don't know if I ever will. But the way you told the story, it felt as if the master was right here, giving his discourse. I promise to live by these teachings for my entire life and to seek out more knowledge. This is the greatest lesson I have ever received."

* * *

RISE OF ABHIMANYU
AND SKY MONK 2

Arjun Singh shared an enthralling story with both Bob and Abhimanyu. While Bob was disinterested and dismissed it, Abhimanyu was captivated and felt enlightened. Driven by a desire to learn more, he delved into the Vedas, Bible, Quran and other ancient texts. He sought out various gurus and masters, but none impressed him. Determined to find the master his father had met, Abhimanyu searched the world.

One day, during deep meditation, Abhimanyu envisioned meeting the master on an airplane while pursuing the metaphorical 'sugar mountain'. A deep, booming voice and a giant monk appeared in his mind, saying,

"Abhimanyu, you are on the right path. Do not be disheartened; you will meet me when the time is right, and it will happen soon." Abhimanyu opened his eyes, tears of joy streaming down his face, feeling ecstatic. He believed he had found the master.

Returning home from his company's annual conclave in Europe, Abhimanyu boarded a flight and was seated in business class. While using the restroom, he overheard a conversation between an air hostess and a pregnant passenger who was requesting a seat change. The air hostess explained that the flight was full but promised to make arrangements after take-off. Abhimanyu offered his business class seat to the pregnant passenger and inquired about her seat. She mentioned seat 7B, a middle seat.

Abhimanyu replied, "I love seat 7B; I usually book 7B. Somehow, my company booked this business class seat."

As Abhimanyu approached seat 7B, he noticed a serene monk in seat 7A.

The monk welcomed him with a booming voice, "I am glad you helped that lady; she truly needed a comfortable seat for the long flight."

Abhimanyu, with tears in his eyes, said, "Master, I have been searching for you all this time. Where have you been?"

The master replied, "I appear at the right time. You must be Arjun Singh's son, Abhimanyu. How is your father? Convey my regards."

Abhimanyu responded, "He is no more; he passed away after sharing his valuable knowledge with society and us."

The master said, "I had blessed him to live for 100 years and more."

Abhimanyu continued, "He lived a blissful and purposeful life, raising us with love. He was one of the saintliest people I have ever known, and I know your contribution. I want to thank you for all that you have done."

Abhimanyu then said, "My father received a grain of sugar from the sugar mountain (the knowledge). I am here for the mountain."

The master replied, "I knew you would come, and it is all yours."

The master said, "I asked for some water, and the air hostess is taking a lot of time to fetch it. I hope she has not gone to the other world to get the water."

Abhimanyu replied, "I have requested water and heard many stories narrated by you to my father, Arjun Singh. I have a lot of questions, and the first one is: How did you disappear from the airport?"

The master said, "It's all maya. Do you know what maya is? I remember a story from the book, *Complete Works of Swami Vivekananda.*"

* * *

"Once, Nârada said to Krishna, 'Lord, show me *Maya*.' A few days passed, and Krishna asked Nârada to make a trip with him toward a desert. After walking for several miles, Krishna said, 'Nârada, I am thirsty; can you fetch some water for me?'

'I will go at once, sir, and get you water,' Nârada said.

So, Nârada went. At a little distance, there was a village. He entered the village in search of water and knocked at a door, which was opened by a most beautiful young girl. At the sight of her, he immediately forgot that his Master was waiting for water, perhaps dying for the want of it.

He forgot everything and began to talk to the girl. All that day, he did not return to his master. The next day, he was again at the house, talking to the girl. That talk ripened into love. He asked the father for the daughter, and they were married. They lived there, had children, and thus twelve years passed.

His father-in-law died, and he inherited his property. He lived, as he seemed to think, a very happy life with his wife, children, fields and cattle. Then came a flood. One night, the river rose, overflowing its banks and flooding the whole village. Houses fell, men and animals were swept away and drowned, and everything was floating in the rush of the stream. Nârada had to escape.

With one hand, he held his wife, and with the other, two of his children. Another child was on his shoulders, and he was trying to ford this tremendous flood. After a few steps, he found the current too strong, and the child on his shoulders fell and was borne away. A cry of despair came from Nârada. In trying to save that child, he lost his grasp on one of the others, and it was also lost. At last, his wife, whom he clasped with all his might, was torn away by the current, and he was thrown onto the bank, weeping and wailing in bitter lamentation.

Behind him, there came a gentle voice. 'My child, where is the water? You went to fetch a pitcher of water, and I am waiting for you; you have been gone for quite half an hour.'

'Half an hour!' Nârada exclaimed. Twelve whole years had passed through his mind, and all these scenes had happened in half an hour! And this is Maya.

The discourse between the master and Abhimanyu reached a new level, and the continuation will be available in *Sky Monk 2*

SOURCES

Complete collection of Swami Vivekananda

Swami Sarva Priyananda

Swami Mukundananda, Bhagavad Gita,

Sadguru, YouTube talk

Mahatria Ra, you tube talk

Robin Sharma, YouTube talk

Dandapani, YouTube talk

Reach the Author for Personal Transformation and Collaboration

Are you looking to transform your personal or professional life? Do you need expert guidance to help your team or community thrive? Look no further! Our author specializes in personal transformation and is eager to collaborate with you.

Personal Coaching and Team Activities

Whether you need one-on-one coaching to unlock your full potential or engaging activities to boost your team's morale and productivity, we are here to help. Our tailored coaching sessions and interactive workshops are designed to meet your unique needs and goals.

Why Choose Us?

- **Expertise**: With years of experience in wellness consulting, NLP, and neuroscience, our author brings a wealth of knowledge and practical insights.

- **Customized Solutions**: We understand that every individual and team is different. Our programs are customized to address your specific challenges and aspirations.

- **Holistic Approach**: We focus on mental health, stress management and overall well-being, ensuring a balanced and fulfilling life.

Get in Touch

We would be more than happy to assist you on your journey to personal and professional growth. Visit our website at www.mentalswitch.in to learn more about our services and to schedule a consultation.

9 7 9 8 8 9 5 5 6 3 8 5 4